Advance Praise for ***We Hug in the Hallways***

"Finding a job that fits you in a company culture that matches your style is absolutely essential to getting the most fulfillment out of your life at work. Understanding both yourself and the people around you are key pieces to this puzzle. ***We Hug in the Hallways Here*** will provide you with helpful insights to finding the combination that works best for you. Roger does an excellent job at sharing his wealth of knowledge and understanding of the DISC profile in a way that is easily understood and leaves you with ideas for taking action. This is a great resource for individuals and professionals alike—in business, in relationships and in life!"

—**Jan Nielsen**, Deputy Executive Director—Human Resources,
Metropolitan Airports Commission, Minneapolis, Minnesota

"Roger Wenschlag has created a wonderful roadmap for anyone concerned about finding the right fit between job and self. Using the powerful DISC model of behavior, he zeros in on motivators and demotivators that can make or break job success and takes the mystery out of organizational culture. Whether you are looking for the perfect job, find yourself in an imperfect job, or guiding others who are, this book is a must read. As a practitioner, I have been using the DISC model for over 20 years and have been waiting for someone to put into book form the essence of matching behavioral style to job demands. This is it!"

—**Rick Stamm**, Founder, The TEAM Approach®

"*We Hug in the Hallways Here* contains a wealth of useful observations and practical tools for the job seeker and for employers that can contribute to more effective job/candidate fit. Wenschlag not only helps candidate's identify roles where they may be most comfortable, but also identifies why. His book is also a great tool for counseling candidates in career transition."

—**Richard Wold**, Executive Vice President,
InSync Northwest

"Roger writes with lucidity and economy of prose while exploring a complex central theme—that understanding and making the most of your personal behavioural style can have a considerable and positive effect on your life and career. It should be required reading for all senior high school students, college undergraduates, and anyone who would benefit from the help and assurance that Roger offers to those considering their future."

—**Tony Reid**, International Training &
Development Associates (UK)

ROGER E. WENSCHLAG'S

We Hug
in the Hallways
Here

ROGER E. WENSCHLAG'S

We Hug
in the Hallways
Here

DISCOVER CAREERS THAT FIT YOUR STYLE

Beaver's
Pond
Press,
Inc.

WE HUG IN THE HALLWAYS HERE © copyright 2008 by Roger E. Wenschlag. All rights reserved. No part of this book may be reproduced in any form whatsoever, by photography or xerography or by any other means, by broadcast or transmission, by translation into any kind of language, nor by recording electronically or otherwise, without permission in writing from the author, except by a reviewer, who may quote brief passages in critical articles or reviews.

All references to DiSC® and DiSC Classical Profile Graphs are used with the permission of Inscape Publishing, Inc. DiSC is a registered trademark of Inscape Publishing, Inc. Copyright 2001. All rights reserved.

ISBN 10: 1-59298-262-X
ISBN 13: 978-1-59298-262-2

Library of Congress Catalog Number: 2008939299

Printed in the United States of America

First Printing: 2009

13 12 11 10 09   5 4 3 2 1

Cover and interior design by James Monroe Design, LLC.

Beaver's Pond Press, Inc.

Beaver's Pond Press, Inc.
7104 Ohms Lane, Suite 101
Edina, MN 55439–2129
(952) 829-8818
www.BeaversPondPress.com

to order, visit www.BookHouseFulfillment.com
or call 1-800-901-3480. Reseller discounts available.

To Diane, my wife of forty-four years,
and my children and grandchildren
for their love and commitment to family.

Note: Throughout the book, I use the generic term *behavioral style* and I use the generic DISC model to explain style. In Chapters 3–6, however, I specifically use Inscape Publishing's trademarked name DiSC®, with the lower-case i. This is because I have used, with their permission, the content and assumptions of their *DiSC® Classical Profile Graphs* in those chapters.

There is an ongoing debate in the DISC-user community about which is better, DISC or DiSC®. Both of these models are similar in their look and terminology, and both have their roots in the same research and practice of the early years. However, over the years, various publishers have made unique changes to and interpretations of the model based on their research and practice.

Contents

Foreword

Every now and then, a book comes along and I ask myself, "Why didn't I write that?" Roger Wenschlag's book *We Hug in the Hallways Here* is one of those. It is about behavioral style—how we express ourselves and deal with others—and how we can use that knowledge to select a career or job and a company in which we fit, and can be at our best. Roger also gives some useful techniques for how to identify the behavioral style of others, and for how to get out of our behavioral comfort zone when necessary, and successfully adapt to people and situations.

I've spent most of my adult life helping people in organizations reach their full potential and achieve higher levels of performance. For all of us, unleashing that potential depends, to a large extent, on how well we know ourselves—our goals, our talents, our values, and our personalities—and can apply that knowledge to maximize our strengths and minimize our limitations. If I've learned anything along the way, one thing is clear: Most of us want to do our best. We want to be in a job and in companies where we experience joy and feel satisfied that we contribute value. This book will help you do that.

The thing I appreciate most about Roger's book is its informal, practical tone. Roger takes a potentially complex subject and makes sense out of it through clear prose, concrete examples, and stories. And there are many opportunities to pause for reflection in the book by answering questions pertaining to your needs and experiences. This makes it easy to read and so useful for job and career search applications. You'll relate well to many of the passages. In fact, throughout the chapter about my style, I found myself saying, "That's me alright!" The book strongly validates what I have known for a long time: When it comes to deciding on a job or career and a place to work, your style does matter!

Roger's book features the DISC model of behavior, a reliable and practical method of describing and understanding human behavior. One of the most interesting parts of the book is the stories of people of the different DISC patterns, in their favorite jobs, telling how they approach their work, and the motivators and demotivators they experience in those jobs. Their thoughts and feelings are brutally honest and insightful. The cases allow us a rare opportunity to peek into their world, and then reflect on how we might feel in similar work.

I hope you enjoy the experience of reading *We Hug in the Hallways Here* as much as I did. Moreover, if you can apply the lessons learned in the book, you can attempt to be in a job within an organization that fits for you. Then you'll have the chance to reach your full potential and experience the joy of work that fits. Good luck.

—**Larry Wilson**, CEO, The Wilson Connection,
founder/past CEO of Wilson Learning Company
and Pecos River Learning Center

Acknowledgements

Through my work as a product manager, consultant, and trainer, I have been a student of behavioral styles and DISC for nearly 30 years. I owe a large debt of gratitude to the hundreds of people I have trained and associated with in this work. Their questions, our discussions, and my observations of their behaviors have provided a rich base of behavioral knowledge that contributed to the book.

I am particularly grateful to my professional colleagues at Inscape Publishing in Minneapolis, Minnesota, for their continuing commitment to produce high-quality assessment materials and training programs, as well as for their gracious permission to use elements of their DiSC® technology in this book.

I am also thankful for my colleagues in the Inscape Publishing distributor network who are daily practitioners of the DiSC® technology. We willingly share ideas, knowledge, and experiences. I have learned a lot from them.

I also want to express my thanks to the many people who participated in the "my favorite job" survey research and interviews that are reflected in the behavioral style case examples in Chapters 3–6. I cannot name them because I agreed to keep them anonymous, but they know who they are. Their real-world testimony of behaviors used in their favorite jobs and their openness about their chief motivators and demotivators are the core of this book. Due to space limitations, I was only able to use 16 of the cases, but all of the participants contributed greatly to my thinking.

In writing this book, I asked 12 people of differing ages and occupations to review a prepublication draft of the book for content and clarity. I want to thank them for their feedback; their comments and suggestions made a big difference in the book's readability and usefulness.

Publishing a book cannot be done without expert help. I owe big thanks to the folks at Beaver's Pond Press—and especially my project manager Dara Moore—for their publishing guidance and support. Also, even though I thought I did a pretty good job of writing, my editor April Michele Davis managed to smooth out several rough edges of the manuscript to make it more readable. I am also indebted to my proofreader, Michele Bassett, for her incredible eye for detail. She made connections and found stuff I didn't even know existed—a wonderful High C! Lastly, I am grateful for having worked with graphic designer Jay Monroe. Through his interpretation of my needs, and his artistry, he took a plain-script manuscript and transformed it into a work of art.

Last, I want to thank my family and close friends who have been my living laboratory to observe and understand behavior. Nearly all of them are in jobs and work cultures that fit for them, so I have been able to talk with them about the purpose and details of the book. They have only confirmed what we all know anyway: Being in a job and work culture that fits one's style is something for which we should try to strive.

Introduction

The idea for this book came from participants in the behavioral style workshops I have taught over the past 20 years. Invariably, not long into the learning, people would ask, "So, what kind of a job would be best for a person with my behavioral style?" or "Where would I fit best?" The short answer is, "You can be effective and satisfied in any job for which you're qualified, BUT…."

This book is about the *but*. It is about the fit between your behavioral style and the requirements of your job. If it is a good fit, chances are you will be both satisfied and happy in your work. If the fit is not so good, you will have to adapt. If that adaptation requires that you get out of your behavioral comfort zone too far and too often, you will likely experience high stress and be ineffective. Let me share an example from my own experience.

Several years ago, while leaving the human resources manager's office on my first day in a new company, she said, "Oh yes, one more thing. We hug in the hallways here." I suppose she saw this as a necessary warning. Actually, I saw it as good news! I like people and enjoy relating to them—even hugging them now and then.

By contrast, I had just left a job in a company where hugging in the hallways would have earned you a spot on the short list of company characters. The culture there was impersonal, formal, and analytical. I am normally an enthusiastic, optimistic, expressive person. My job as a training manager there had its positive moments, where I could be myself, but if I wanted to be taken seriously I had to perform my job in a manner that was quite unnatural for me. Long term, this adaptation took its toll—I had lost touch with myself and was unhappy. Finally, I quit. In the new job (after a few hugs in the hallways), I quickly recovered and got in touch with the real me.

As implied in my example, there are two aspects of one's work associated with behavioral style and job satisfaction and effectiveness: workgroup culture and job-role requirements. If you are in a workgroup culture that fits your style, chances are you will be happy. For example, if you are an active, assertive, hard-driving person and your coworkers are the same way, you will feel at home. However, if you are a more deliberate, methodical, analytical person, you will likely feel some level of stress in a culture like this.

In addition to work culture, the other aspect of work linked to job satisfaction and effectiveness is job-role requirements. If your various job roles require behaviors from you that are natural and comfortable, chances are you will be satisfied and productive. Conversely, if you have to constantly stretch and redirect your behavior to meet the role requirements of your job, you will probably feel some level of stress and not be as productive.

This book is about the fit between your behavioral style and the requirements of your job, and it is about how to use that knowledge to select a career or find a job where you can be the most satisfied and productive. Put yourself into the situations I have written about, and apply what you learned to your own situation. By doing so, I hope that you too can find an increased level of job satisfaction and effectiveness.

Ultimately, if I can help you make a good decision, or help you avoid making a bad one, I will have succeeded in my goal. In addition, if you are in a job that is a bad fit you may understand your situation better and work to improve things. I also think this book could help you improve your working relationships with others by helping you understand, appreciate, and value them regardless of your differences.

About the Author

Since I am giving information and advice about making job and career choices in this book, I thought it would be helpful for you to know more about me as a person. Therefore, I will give you a brief autobiography, with emphasis on my own jobs and career development over the years. As you read about my preferences and experiences, see if you can detect the connection between my behavioral pattern and needs, and the kind of work I have performed over the years.

I was born in 1941 and raised in a working-class family in south Minneapolis, Minnesota. My father was a heavy machinery mover, and my mother was a homemaker, taking care of us three kids. As far back as I can remember, I was always a social kid, with an independent streak. I had many friends and enjoyed being around people, both children and adults. I was ambitious and had many early jobs such as shoveling snow, mowing lawns, and delivering newspapers. I learned early the value and importance of doing good work. For fun, I enjoyed taking long bike rides to explore the city and its many parks and lakes. In the fifth and sixth grades, I ran the film projector for various teachers in the school. In the sixth grade, I served as our school patrol captain, responsible for the proper performance of our student street-crossing guards. *Can you see a behavior pattern forming here?*

As a 14-year-old, my first real part-time job was working for my dad as a service station attendant. I pumped gas; fixed tires; and greased, oiled, and washed cars. My favorite part of the job was talking to customers. I enjoyed the interaction and learning more about them. Later, during my high school years, I worked in a car wash. I was the greeter at the back door, where people drove in and left their cars to be washed. After awhile I knew most of our customers. Again, I enjoyed this work because it involved connecting with people and serving them.

In high school, I was popular, but not because of sports or any particular talent. I guess I stood out because of my height (6' 5") and my efforts to be friendly and get along with others. As a tenth grader, I read Dale Carnegie's *How to Win Friends and Influence People,* the classic book about leadership and influence. It was a revelation to me because up until then I had unknowingly applied many of Carnegie's principles in my own young life. I felt validated! As a high schooler, I was capable of doing good academic work, but chose easy courses just to get by. I was demotivated and bored with most of my classes, but enjoyed the social side of school. From the greasers, to the jocks, to the bookworms, I prided myself in having a foothold and friends in all of those camps. As a result, I was elected to many student leadership posts, such as student council representative and senior executive board. I enjoyed the exposure, responsibilities, and relationships of those activities. *Do you see a behavior pattern here?*

From a development perspective, one of the most changing events of my life occurred in the twelfth grade when I joined the U.S. Naval Reserve. I saw purpose, direction, and an opportunity to get involved in something important and exciting. Immediately after high school graduation, I participated in a 90-day recruit boot camp and aviation apprentice-training program. Because, by then, I had been in the Navy longer than most of the other recruits, the Command CPO selected me to be the recruit chief petty officer, responsible for leading 40 other sailors in my section. I was also in the recruit color guard and the recruit choir. We participated in several community parades and festivals. It was a busy and fulfilling summer. I enjoyed the formal leadership role, the varied activities, and the chance to build relationships. These opportunities were consistent with my need for responsibility, variety, influence, and exposure.

For the next eight years, I served in the U.S. Navy as an aircraft mechanic, leadership instructor, and shop supervisor. The common theme throughout this time was hard work, responsibility, and leadership by example. I received regular promotions and recognition for various achievements along the way. My favorite part of being a Navy petty officer was directing things, leading sailors, and influencing them to do their best. The most difficult part of leadership for me was standing firm on some issue or getting tough with chronic non-performers. After all, I wanted positive relationships and to be liked by others. Upon discharge from active service, I joined the Naval Reserve again and continued with the Navy until I retired after 26 years of service. One of the highlights of my reserve service was serving as a full-time Navy recruiter during two summers. The job required meeting people, influencing them positively about the Navy, and persuading them to sign up. *Do you see a behavior pattern here?*

After my discharge from active naval service, I attended college at the University of Minnesota where I earned a BS in sales and marketing education, and then eventually an MS in vocational education, with an emphasis on career development. I wanted to be a teacher because I liked business and I enjoyed my teaching experience from my Navy days. In addition, I liked young people; I thought I could make a difference for them. Throughout college, I was involved in many student leadership activities. I enjoyed being in charge and influencing others in a positive way.

After graduating from college, I joined the staff of a new high school where I taught a sales and marketing cooperative education program. My students worked part-time in the local community and took related classes in school. The job required building strong relationships with the business community, the students' parents, the students, and the school staff. Most of all, I enjoyed leading and influencing the kids to succeed. My favorite part of the work was mentoring, coaching, and supporting individuals. After teaching for two years, I moved into vocational school administration where I served briefly as department head, and then as a school director for nine years. I led a staff of 21 teachers. I was also active in our state vocational directors' association professional activities, serving as state president for a term. These administrative jobs required a high level of involvement, influence, and leadership. I enjoyed them because of the personal relationships, the independence of the work, and the chance to make a difference for others. *Do you see a behavioral pattern here?*

During the next stage of my career, I left vocational education for the world of training and development in the business sector. I served as the training director in two companies, and then as a product manager and a sales training director for a global training company. All these jobs required a strong people orientation, good communications, and the ability to get things done. I thrived in this kind of work. Eventually, in 1989 I started a small training and consulting firm. Being self-employed served my need for service to others, variety, independence, and adequate financial rewards.

So, after reading about my career, what behavioral pattern(s) did you see in me? What do you think I liked about my work? If you saw in me a high degree of people and results orientation, you are right. In fact, my measured style is Persuader, a combination of a High I and D, and a moderately High S. I have no C! You will soon learn about these behavioral patterns in Chapters 3–6.

Regarding my own career, I have been lucky to be in jobs that brought out the best of my skills and abilities and that allowed me to capitalize on my behavioral style strengths. Most of my jobs were a good fit. I hope the same for you.

Obtain Your Own DISC Behavioral Style Report

This book will be most interesting and relevant if you have your own behavioral style report. It will give you a reliable and useful perspective of your own style as you read and apply the chapters in the book. To get your own behavioral style report, go to www.WeHugintheHallwaysHere.com, where you will find a full description of the DISC behavioral style report. You can complete it online and download it in about half an hour. You will find the tool to be fun, interesting, and revealing. Most importantly, the style report will help you understand your style well enough to be able to apply that information in your career choices and in your current job.

Chapter Summaries

Let us look at a summary of each chapter in the book to see where this learning journey will take you.

ONE: A Near Perfect Fit
Working in a Job Where There Is Some Hope for Joy

In this chapter, you will learn the general framework of making a good job choice, i.e., skills, abilities, values, and the role that your personal style plays in that mix. Then, we will dig a little deeper into job culture, job-role requirements, and job fit.

TWO: DISC Behavioral Styles
Everyone Has One, So What?

This chapter features the background and fundamentals of behavioral style and outlines specifics of the DISC behavioral style model, which consists of four distinctly different style tendencies—Dominance, Influence, Steadiness, and Conscientiousness. You will learn about the origins of these DISC behaviors and the characteristics of each.

In the following chapter summaries and throughout the book, I use the terms "High D," "High I," "High S," and "High C." This is simply a shorthand way of saying that if we gave someone the DISC assessment, and they came out very high in one of the DISC behavioral tendencies compared to the other dimensions, we would refer to them as a "High X." This is not to say that people have only a limited behavioral range, i.e., that of a single high dimension. On the contrary, we apply a full range of behaviors in expressing our distinctive personalities.

Note: Chapters 3–6 cover each of the DISC behavioral dimensions in depth, including the subtleties of what motivates and demotivates people of each style and how they typically affect others. You will also learn about specific jobs (and cultures) that are a good match for each style, and we will cover the jobs and situations that would be demotivating. This knowledge will help you make better choices about what kind of work you might want to do and where you might be happiest working. In addition, you will find some good tips about how to deal more effectively with people of each of these respective styles if their style is different from yours.

THREE: The High D:

"Give me a challenge and get out of the way!"

This chapter will give you insights about people who have the High D, Dominance, style. These kinds of people thrive on producing results through control over their environments.

FOUR: The High I:

"No matter what, I've got to work with people who are enthusiastic and interactive!"

Here you will learn about people who have the High I, Influence, style. High Is thrive on relationships formed through their persuading and influencing skills.

FIVE: The High S:

"Let's work together and get this done in a calm and effective manner!"

This chapter will give you information about people who have the High S, Steadiness, style. They are happiest when they are able to achieve stable and predictable work environments.

SIX: The High C:

"Before we take action on this I want to assess the pros and cons to be sure I make the right decision!"

In this chapter, you will gain valuable information about people who have the High C, Conscientiousness, style. These people thrive in situations where they can set and achieve high standards of work.

SEVEN: Practicing Adaptability:

"To be or not to be? That is the question ... and the opportunity."

It is a fact: People who can adapt their personal style to meet the needs of others in various situations are a prized resource in organizations. In this chapter, we will make a case for leaving your comfort zone and for being more adaptive with others. We will also give you a tool for planning your adaptability strategy, as well as specific techniques for being more flexible.

ONE

A Near Perfect Fit:
Working in a Job Where There Is Some Hope for Joy

The Challenge of Making the Right Job or Career Choice

"So, what do you want to do when you grow up?" When posed to little children, this time-honored question usually evokes a predictable response: "a police officer," "a fireman," "a teacher." Kids choose these jobs because they still live in a small world and they are most familiar with the community helpers who are featured in children's books and on television.

Recently I asked my five-year-old grandson the same question. Expecting to hear one of these predictable responses, I was a bit surprised when he quickly said, "I want to be a boss." I asked, "Why?" He said, "So I can tell other people what to do." (Oh, if career and job selection could be so easy!) What happened here? Somewhere in his intellectual and emotional framework, he sensed that being in charge would agree with him. In fact, his response was entirely consistent with the behaviors I have observed in him lately. Even at five, he seems to be developing into a dominant, assertive little person—a High D.

What will his answer be to the same question 16 or so years from now? I don't know, but his answer probably will not come as quickly or as easily as now. That is because most young people who are about to embark on their own have considerable anguish about picking a college major, a career field, or that first job. The lucky ones have had the benefit of good counseling at home and in school, and through part-time work. Even for them the job and career choice issue is a big deal. Do you remember your own experience with this dilemma? How did you decide? With whom did you talk? What factors did you consider when you decided what to do?

Career experts suggest that we should define ourselves by *who we are*, not by *what we do*. That is a good guideline for happy living, but the work we choose is also hugely important because so much of our self-concept, happiness, and job satisfaction are rooted in what we do. A good friend of mine, who spent his entire career as a vocational/career educator, says it best: "What we do is who we are, and a good part of what we do is our career." If you don't believe that, ask people how painful it is when they have jobs where they are square pegs in round holes. Is it any wonder that Richard Bolles's book for job-hunters and career-changers, *What Color Is Your Parachute?*, has been a best seller for over 35 years?

When it came to choosing my career path, I was one of the lucky ones. Throughout my teens, I had many jobs and experiences—from farm work, to retailing, to service station work, to car washing—where I could see the world of work and assess how I might fit in. In addition, I was around many adults in the workplace. It was fun and enlightening to see how they interacted with each other and dealt with their daily challenges and issues. All of these experiences were a great help for me in discovering what I liked and did not like. Then, when I joined the Navy Reserve in the twelfth grade, I had the added benefit of comprehensive testing and classification services. By that time, I knew who I was and what I wanted. As my life and career evolved over time, I continued to rely on Navy and college counseling resources and other tools to make sure I was going in the right direction. Looking back on things, I can say that, for the most part, I was fortunate to be in good-fit jobs and work cultures where I could be happy and productive.

Important Things to Consider in Job or Career Choice

What are the things that we should consider when making a decision about which career or job to pursue? The answer may vary with individuals, but there is common agreement among most career experts and writers that there are several key factors to consider. Since the scope of this book is about your behavior style and your job or career, I will only summarize those other factors here:

- *Skills*: Skills are the abilities and talents we have that allow us to perform at our best. Some skills are natural, such as cognitive memory or the ability to relate to people. You can learn other skills such as reading a blueprint or performing a delicate operation. What are your abilities and talents? What experiences have you had where you enjoyed them and excelled? What are you able to do? What do you like best—working with data, people, or things?

- *Values*: Do you have a strong mission or purpose related to your job or career? What do you care about most in your work? What kind of work would be motivating to you? What do you want to do; what do you not want to do?

- *Interests*: If you did what you loved, and the money would follow, what would capture your interest? What are your hobbies? What would you do, even if you had to work for free? What kind of people or activities attract you?

- *Financial*: How much money do you want to make? What are you willing to do to prepare for this? Do you have the skills and temperament for the kind of work necessary to make the kind of money you want?

- *Behavioral Style*: How do you prefer to interact with the world around you? What is your behavioral style? What are your behavioral strengths and limitations? What kinds of work would be a good fit for your personality? What kinds of work environments (culture) would you find motivating? Where would you be demotivated and frustrated?

If you are in the personal discovery mode and looking for more in-depth information about your job skills and other career-related issues, you may wish to consult your company's human resources department or a school counselor, take a career exploration class commonly offered at community colleges, search the Internet, or read a couple of books on the subject. Two of my favorite books are the following:

- *What Color is Your Parachute?*, Ten Speed Press, by Richard Bolles. This book is a practical manual for job hunters and career changers.

- *Discover What You're Best At*, Fireside Book, Simon and Shuster, by Linda Gale. This book offers a series of aptitude tests that will help you discover your true career abilities, and it suggests, by education level, typical careers that would fit your skills.

The Role of Behavioral Style in Your Job or Career Choice

How often have you heard someone say, "So-and-so should go into sales. She is so outgoing and such a great talker!" or "So-and-so should consider being an accountant. He is so detail-oriented and analytical." No doubt, you've heard other such comments as they might apply to other job fields as well. Are these just common occupational stereotypes, or is there a grain of truth in them?

My experience and research with behavioral style says that there is more truth than fiction here. This is because every job requires certain behaviors from the jobholder if that person is to be successful in that job. Therefore, looking at the above examples, it is a fact—most sales jobs require that the salesperson be outgoing and persuasive. As well, to be a successful accountant, it helps to be detail-oriented and analytical. These, and dozens of other behavioral characteristics, can be easily recognized and understood when we put them in the framework of behavioral style. So, what is behavioral style and why is it so important?

Our behavioral style is how we prefer to interact with our environment and the people around us. Our style is a function of many factors, most notably our internal emotions—the goals and fears that motivate or demotivate us based on what is happening around us. For example:

- If you are a person with a strong need to achieve and produce results (High D goals), you would typically interact with your world in a direct and controlling manner. If you sense that you are about to lose control (a High D fear), you might even escalate your level of control to assure that you come out on top. This is one of my moderately high behaviors.

- If you are a person with a strong need to be involved with people and make a favorable impression (High I goals), you would likely relate to your world in an outgoing, enthusiastic manner. If you experience any social rejection, disapproval, or loss of influence (a High I fear), you might react by displaying more verbal expression and heightened emotion. You might even leave the scene to avoid looking bad. I have a high degree of this behavior pattern.

- If you have a strong need to maintain stability and harmony (High S goals) in your world, you would probably interact with your world in a cooperative and friendly way. Any threat to these goals, such as sudden change or disharmony (High S fears), would likely cause you to react initially by going along with things to avoid conflict. Eventually, because of internal pressure and resentment, you might come out and behave more aggressively. I have a moderate level of this behavior.

- If you have a strong need for clear direction, high standards, quality, and accuracy (High C goals), you would typically respond to your world in a diplomatic, precise, and analytical manner. Any threat to your goals, such as criticism by others, or a disorganized work environment (High C fears), would typically cause you to get quiet and fix things. In doing so you would probably even avoid future contacts with such people or situations until you have built a case showing how right you are. I consistently score very low in this behavioral tendency.

The emotions that drive us show up in a predictable set of surface behaviors and characteristics that we display to others, more or less consistently, as we go about our day-to-day activities. This is known as our behavioral style. These behaviors are those most comfortable for us—they are habitual. We call them our comfort zone. In general, we express the behaviors through

- our body language (gestures, facial expressions, posture, and pace)
- our voice tone (volume, pace, and inflection)
- the messages we deliver (priorities, focus, and approaches).

When you are able to work in a job and a work culture that meet your needs, you are typically happier, less stressed, and more productive. You can be satisfied and productive in *any* job, no matter what your style. However, you must be prepared to adapt to the various roles required in your job. This is important because some jobs or roles may require more flexibility from you than you are prepared to give.

The Role of Values in Our Behavior

Before moving on, we need to discuss briefly the role that values play in our behavior. Values are the beliefs we hold that heavily influence our behavior; they are the standards by which we live our lives. In organizations, values are the "thou shalts," and the "thou shalt nots" that determine the way we work with each other, our customers, our suppliers, and others. For example, you may believe in fair play, so regardless of your own emotional needs, you would act in ways to assure that others get fair treatment. As another example, suppose you were in a heated meeting and wanted to unload your emotions, but did not because you believe that it is important to respect others. Going further, if you value hard work, then in spite of other factors, you would typically commit to getting things done, no matter what the costs in time and energy. Our values are a product of our national culture, our upbringing, and our institutions, including work.

Values play a critical role in our behavior because they usually serve to screen our natural, goal-driven, and fear-driven behaviors. They represent the rational, thinking side of our behavior. However, sometimes our emotions are so strong that we go around the values and act purely from emotion. Depending on our makeup and the circumstances, our natural urge may be to fight through direct, aggressive behavior or to take flight by shutting down, or giving in to others. We are not at our best when we act out of emotion. When things have cooled down, we usually have to make things right with others who may have been on the receiving end of our reactive behavior.

Role Flexibility

It would be nice if you could perform your job all day, every day, within your behavioral comfort zone, but that is unlikely to happen. The fact is, no matter what your style, to be effective you must always adapt your behavior to meet the different role requirements of your job. In other words, no matter how much you would like to do the job in a way that makes you more comfortable, you will often need to be adaptive and perform it in a way that will produce the best results. We call this *role flexibility*. It should come as no surprise to you: People who consistently show high levels of role flexibility are the most highly prized by their organizations.

As an example, let us look at role flexibility for the job of a customer service manager. The typical roles of this job are employee coach/mentor, customer problem solver, financial budget manager, and department leader. Each role requires a different mix of behavior:

- The role of coach/mentor requires open, honest feedback, empathic listening, supportiveness, and directive management.

- The role of customer problem solver requires patience, good listening, assertiveness, and emotional control.
- The role of financial budget manager requires attention to detail, patience, accuracy, and unswerving judgment.
- The role of department leader requires results orientation, collaborative goal setting, good two-way communications and listening, vision and clarity about department goals, enthusiasm, and support for others.

Depending on your natural behavioral style you might be very comfortable with some aspects of these roles, and quite uncomfortable with others. For example, someone with a high level of dominance (D) behavior would likely enjoy the role of department leader because it requires a fair amount of goal setting, direction, and control. We call that a *fit* because these are typically a High D's strengths. The same role also calls for good two-way communication and listening, something High Ds typically have to work on to be effective. This is a *stretch*. The role also requires collaborative goal setting. Since the typical High D is most comfortable telling and controlling, in this role the leader would have to guard against this instinct and allow others to contribute their ideas. This requires one to *redirect* a strength.

Given the unique characteristics of each behavioral style, you could go back and make the same analysis for each style, for each role. Do you know what you would discover?

- Some roles are natural for us; they just seem to fit.
- Some roles require that we stretch out of our comfort zone to be effective. We have to do things that are stressful, that make us uncomfortable.
- Some roles require us to redirect a strength so we do not overdo it. This too requires our energy and commitment.

Therefore, if you can find work in a job and an organizational culture that is a reasonably good fit with your style, you are likely to experience more satisfaction, less stress, and higher productivity.

Chapter Summary

Choosing a career or new job is an exciting, yet somewhat frightening process. We want to make the right decision that leads to happy and productive work, but we know there are no guarantees. That is why it is so important that we know ourselves—our goals, interests, skills, capabilities, values, and behavioral style before we decide. The better the fit on these, the better our chances of success. Of all of these, our behavioral style should be at or near the top as a factor in making career and job choices. This is because, ideally, in a good-fit situation we would be well suited to perform the various roles of a job and make the adjustments needed to perform effectively. We would then likely experience more satisfaction, less stress, and higher productivity. Conversely, if we are unable to adjust, and the job takes us too far out of our behavioral comfort zone too often, we would likely be stressed out, and would probably be unproductive. Our work relationships would also suffer.

Some Things to Think About

What jobs have you considered in which you thought you might be effective? What are they? What appeals to you? Do any of these appeals have anything to do with your behavioral style?

_____

_____

_____

Has anyone ever told you that you should consider a certain job because you exhibit certain behaviors? What behaviors? What job did they mention? What do you think are the role requirements of that job?

_____

_____

_____

In your work experience, which of your jobs have been a good fit for your behavioral style? Why? Which role(s) within your job(s) were most comfortable for you to perform? Why?

_____

_____

_____

Have you ever had a job that was *not* a good fit for your behavioral style? What job was it? What role(s) required you to stretch or moderate your behaviors to be most effective? How did these adaptations affect your stress level?

_____

_____

_____

Have you ever worked in an organization where you felt comfortable within that culture (how they interacted and the way they did things)? What was it about the culture that appealed to you? How did this affect your happiness and productivity?

_____

_____

_____

Have you ever worked in an organization where you felt uncomfortable within the culture? What was it about the culture that you did not like? How did this affect your happiness and productivity?

_____

_____

_____

Have you ever worked in an organization where various supervisor(s) expected different behaviors from you in your performance of the same role? What was it like for you?

_____

_____

_____

DISC Behavioral Styles:
Everyone Has One, So What?

The Origins of Behavioral Style Thinking

As noted in Chapter 1, under normal circumstances most people approach life in predictable ways. Our behavioral style, or temperament, is evident to others in what we say, in how we say it, and in our body language. Throughout history, many thinkers and writers have attempted to explain the behavioral differences that they observed in people. The most important of these observers were the following:

- Hippocrates, in ancient Greece, described four substances called humours that, when in balance, create a healthy person. The humours were blood, phlegm, yellow bile, and black bile. Later, Theophrastus and others developed a set of characters based on these humours. Those with too much blood were sanguine (a High I tendency). Those with too much phlegm were phlegmatic (a High C tendency). Those with too much yellow bile were choleric (a High D tendency), and those with too much black bile were melancholic (a High S tendency). These temperaments, or styles, shaped the thinking and writing of philosophers, scientists, and writers for centuries.

- Dr. Carl Jung, in 1924, wrote a more scientific view of behavioral style in *Personality Types*. He described four distinct styles: Intuitor, Thinker, Feeler, and Sensor. Jung's work led to many important psychological works and assessments.

- Dr. William Marston, in his 1920s book, *The Emotions of Normal People*, described four tendencies of behavior: dominance, inducement, submissiveness, and compliance. With further research and adaptations over the years, Marston's work led to the development of the DISC behavioral model, the style model I have used in this book.

All of these style models have two things in common: They all group our behavior into four categories, and they are helpful in understanding our behavioral differences. There is one distinction worth noting here. Most style models, including Hippocrates's and Jung's, explain our behavior as *internal characteristics that lead to external behaviors*. Marston's model focuses on *external patterns of observable behaviors that represent internal emotions*. Both models are valid, useful, and widely applied in organizational settings. Because our DISC patterns are reflected in our external behavior, they are easier to read, and thus, DISC is an easier model for others to understand us.

Marston's DISC Model of Behavior

Marston created the early DISC style names and definitions when he theorized that we can define human behavior by framing it on a two-axis model as noted below. (**Note:** I have simplified Marston's actual model to make it easier to understand.) If you understand the dynamics of this model, you will be miles ahead in understanding your and others' behaviors. It really is the key to the safe in terms of knowledge worth knowing.

In Figure 2.1, on the horizontal continuum, Marston discovered that people view their world in two completely different ways. Those on the right tend to see their world as supportive and favorable to themselves (Ss and Is). They prefer to affiliate with others. People on the left tend to see the world as less supportive and unfavorable to themselves (Ds and Cs). They prefer to detach from others. Because of the emotions driving the behaviors, these different views result in distinctly different behaviors. Neither view is right nor wrong, just different.

Those at the **left**, who see the world as more unfavorable and unsupportive to themselves and prefer detachment, typically have a tendency to

- be questioning, logical, objective, skeptical, and challenging
- create and maintain secure boundaries
- create and maintain a separate identity
- value personal space and privacy
- value independence and autonomy
- value being original and creative.

Those at the **right**, who see the world as more favorable and supportive to themselves and prefer affiliation, typically have a tendency to

- be accepting, people-focused, empathetic, receptive, and agreeable

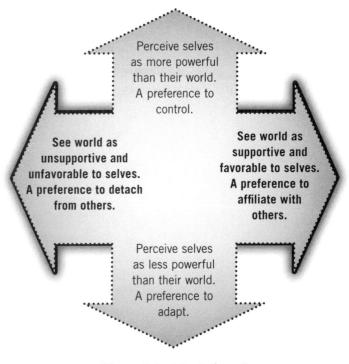

Figure 2.1. Adaptation of William Marston's Model

- be involved in doing things with others
- talk, share, and exchange ideas with others
- reveal, disclose, and share information with others
- seek approval from others.

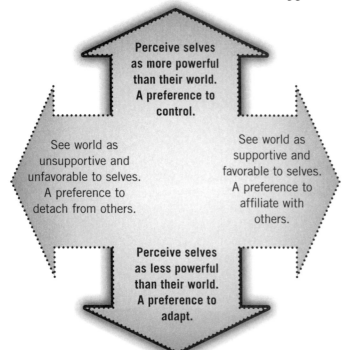

Figure 2.1. Adaptation of William Marston's Model

On the vertical continuum, Marston described the differences in how people sense the extent of power they have over their environment. People on the top (Ds and Is) tend to see themselves as more powerful than their environment. They prefer to exercise control over people and situations. Those at the bottom of the continuum (Cs and Ss) tend to see themselves as less powerful. They prefer to adapt to people and situations. These different views result in distinctly different behaviors as well. Again, neither view is right nor wrong, just different.

Those at the **top**, who see themselves as more powerful than their environment and prefer to control people and situations, have a tendency to

- be active, fast-paced, assertive, dynamic, and bold
- assume responsibility for others, outcomes, and results
- set an example for others
- lead, guide, and teach
- advise, support, and protect
- encourage and direct others.

Those at the **bottom**, who see themselves as less powerful than their environment and prefer to adapt to people and situations, have a tendency to

- be thoughtful, moderate-paced, calm, methodical, and careful
- trust and respect others

- rely and depend upon others
- seek direction and guidance from others
- feel comfortable in adapting to others.

Before proceeding, I must sound a note of caution about seeing ourselves within this framework of Marston's model. We must apply the model in the context of our daily lives. Every day we experience a wide range of people and situations that color our view and emotions. At any given time, we may appear behaviorally any place on the horizontal or vertical continuums.

For example, there are times when we feel quite comfortable with the situations and people around us. We don't feel threatened. Because of this, we will typically show a wider range of behavior as shown on this model. We can safely move around the model showing a wide range of behaviors.

However, some situations and people evoke in us a higher level of emotional tension because we are not comfortable with things as they are. We feel threatened because we are not getting our emotional needs met. These situations typically cause us to go strongly and squarely to our comfort zone, where we feel safest. At times like this we are less flexible and go overboard in showing our style, often to our detriment. Under these conditions, we don't move around much in the model.

As an example of this situational behavior, one of my best friends has a controlling, detached style of personality (D, C). When dining in a restaurant with him, he is quite outgoing, sociable, and fun—until the food is late or cold! Then, seeing a situation unfavorable to himself and feeling more powerful than his world, he will display a distinct change in his behavior to a more detached, controlling style to fix what is wrong. The message to the server, in a very commanding way is, "Nothing personal here, just get it done right ... now!"

At this same meal, another member of the party would see things completely differently. She tends to see the world as a friendly, supportive place. She is a High S and likes people. She also prefers to adapt, living within circumstances, rather than overpowering others. When her food is late, or cold, she would approach things very differently. She would have a tendency to say nothing, or at the very least, only complain to those of us in the dinner party. The message is, "Let's just get along here. So the food is late (or cold)—maybe they're short of cooks tonight."

The Four Behavioral Style Tendencies

Now, given Marston's model, what are the four style tendencies and what are their characteristics? Knowing this, especially your own unique style, will help you answer those two burning career questions:

- Given my style, in what kind of a job will I likely experience satisfaction and effectiveness?
- In what kind of a work culture will I feel most at home?

We will go into much more depth on each of the four styles in the next four chapters of the book, but for now let me introduce them. Each of the four behavioral tendencies is distinct and noticeable. The range of behaviors and characteristics described in Table 2.1 for each of the style tendencies will help you come to some tentative conclusions about which you are. Check or highlight the characteristics that are most like you. The styles are easy to observe in our behaviors:

- **Dominant (D)** style people are determined, straightforward, and motivated by challenging opportunities and by producing results. People who display this approach tend to overcome unfavorable obstacles that block their way. They like competition. They tend to be assertive, independent, decisive, and direct. They get demotivated when others try to control them or take advantage of them in any way. They tend to thrive in jobs and environments where they are in charge and can take responsibility for producing results.

- Another unique expression of behavior is the **Influence (I)** tendency. People of this style tend to focus their energies on influencing or persuading others in favorable situations. They tend to be optimistic, emotional, talkative, and eager to please, and they seek social recognition. They become demotivated when they lose the recognition and approval of others. They tend to thrive in jobs and environments where they can interact with others and influence them through persuasion.

- People of the **Steadiness (S)** style tend to go along with others. They are low-keyed, easygoing, and typically follow through on matters because of their high need for stability. They tend to be good listeners and strive to maintain calm and peaceful relationships with others. Conflict and sudden change can be very demotivating to them because that tends to threaten their stability. People of this style tend to thrive in jobs and environments where they can serve others and contribute their specialized skills for the good of the organization.

- The fourth tendency is **Conscientiousness (C)**. People with a natural C like things done the right or correct way, as *they* see it. They show a high level of caution that fulfills their personal concern for accuracy. They tend to be very dependable and follow through on their agreements. They tend to act in ways that meet their own high standards of appropriate behavior and strive to reduce antagonistic factors that they would tend to see in an unfavorable environment. Personal criticism and sloppy work by others are big demotivators for the High C. They tend to thrive in jobs and environments where they can be accurate and show their expertise.

Table 2.1. Summary of DISC Behavioral Tendencies

CHARACTERISTIC	DOMINANCE	INFLUENCE	STEADINESS	CONSCIENTIOUSNESS
Most Recognizable Behaviors	• Direct • Interrupts • High Strung • Cool, serious • Faster paced • Action-oriented • Decisive • Phone: Succinct	• Expressive • Easily distracted • Warm, friendly • Informal • Faster paced • Spontaneous • Enthusiastic • Phone: Talkative	• Low-key • Agreeable • Warm, calm • Patient • Moderate paced • Indirect • Empathetic • Phone: Friendly	• Deliberate • Critical • Dependable • Cool, formal • Systematic • Logical • Moderate paced • Phone: Organized
Motivated Most by	• Results • Winning • Control	• Recognition • The chase • Others' approval	• Stability • Involvement • Friendships	• Accuracy • The process • Thoroughness
Demotivated Most by	• Loss of control • Being conned	• Loss of approval • Loss of prestige	• Loss of stability • Sudden change	• Personal criticism • Disorder
Typical Strengths	• Accepts challenges • Focus on results and bottom line • Self-motivated • Solves problems • Quick to decide • Challenges the status quo	• Optimistic view of people and situations • Initiates relationships • Motivates others • Persuasiveness • Enthusiastic • Moves quickly with energy	• Dependable and loyal team worker • Consistent and predictable • Helps others • Shows patience • Creates stable, harmonious work environment • Good listener	• Non-emotional decision maker • Conscientious • Systematic • Maintains standards • Detail-oriented • Analyzes performance critically
Typical Limitations	• Overuses impatience • Lack of concern for others • Overly blunt in communications • High strung, not relaxed • Reacts strongly when challenged	• Impulsive decision maker • Disorganized • Exaggerates conditions or facts • Overly concerned with feelings of others • Loss of emotional control	• Overly willing to give in to others • Resistant to positive change • Reluctant to speak out • Overly kind and tolerant • Procrastinates	• Overly critical of self and others • Indecisive due to need for more data • Creativity hampered by need to follow the rules • Prefers facts over feelings • Overly serious

CHARACTERISTIC	DOMINANCE	INFLUENCE	STEADINESS	CONSCIENTIOUSNESS
Most Favorable Workplaces and Jobs Are Where They Can	• *Be independent* • *Make decisions* • *Be direct* • *Compete and achieve* • *Produce results*	• *Be with others* • *Be enthusiastic* • *Be optimistic* • *Solve problems with others* • *Have variety*	• *Be cooperative* • *Show loyalty* • *Act with humility* • *Demonstrate thoughtfulness* • *Work in a team*	• *Be accurate* • *Do things completely* • *Be detailed* • *Follow schedules* • *Be dependable*
Most Unfavorable Workplaces and Jobs Are Where	• *People are too sensitive* • *There is undue hesitation* • *Decisions are overanalyzed* • *People fail to act* • *Weakness is shown*	• *Rules dominate* • *People are too cautious* • *Analysis is favored over action* • *Feelings are ignored* • *People are quiet and introverted*	• *Conflict abounds* • *It is disruptive and noisy* • *Behavior is nonconforming* • *Unsteadiness prevails* • *People are pushy*	• *Mistakes are tolerated* • *Illogical decisions are made* • *People are late, and sloppy with time* • *Careless research is conducted* • *There are sudden deadlines*

The first practical application of the DISC model came during World War II when the U.S. military inducted millions of men and women into the services. Along with vocational aptitude tests, the DISC profile of new recruits provided an additional useful tool for putting them into the right assignments. For example, the Army probably would not have placed a person with a Low C in the job of company clerk because such a job requires high accuracy and a strong attention to detail—High C characteristics. Likewise, the Army probably would not have placed a person with a Low D in the job of provost (a military police chief) because this type of a job requires a high level of action orientation and decisiveness—High D characteristics.

Recognizing these DISC behavioral tendencies is quite useful in understanding others and ourselves, but we need to be cautious. It is very easy just to look at someone's behavior, organize it in our mind, and then put them into a behavioral pigeon hole. However, humans are more complex than that. In fact, about 75 percent of us have a natural behavioral style that incorporates at least two of these DISC tendencies, sometimes even three of them. Only about 25 percent of the population consistently shows only one DISC tendency, i.e., a pure D, I, S, or C style. We can only be very accurate in our style reading if we observe a person's DISC behaviors in a variety of settings over time.

Another interesting and useful part of knowing DISC is its relationship to intuition. For example, when we sense something around us and it involves behavior, DISC provides us with a ready-made set of rules that explain why others do what they do and how we can use that knowledge to optimize our intuition.

Often people ask, "Is my DISC pattern my whole personality, or is there more?" The short answer is, "Yes, there is more." Going back to Marston's model, DISC is a behavioral expression of our internal emotions in response to situations around us. Our total personality consists of so many other things and certainly influences our DISC behaviors. These include inborn traits, mental capacity and how we express it, energy level, life experiences, cultural values and beliefs, and skills and abilities.

A Final Word about Behavioral Style Models

Researchers and publishers have created several behavioral style models since the 1950s. Although they have different names, e.g., social styles, behavior colors, and DISC, they all have one thing in common: They describe how we express our internal emotions through our external behavior.

Chapter Summary

We all have a behavioral style. Our styles are a blend of the behaviors we use to meet the needs and requirements of the situations of our daily lives. Our behavior is a reflection of our emotions—how we feel about our world and about the sense of power we have within that world. We are usually most comfortable with others and ourselves when we are able to achieve our emotional goals and when we are able to avoid our fears. If we feel threatened in any way, we become tense and act more out of fear and raw emotion. At such times, we are least flexible in our behaviors.

Knowing our behavioral styles and preferences can give us important clues about what kind of jobs and work environments would be most suitable. In the following chapters, we will explore the specifics of this important aspect of career choice.

Some Things to Think About

As you read this chapter, were you able to determine your own style? What are your most dominant tendencies?

_____

_____

_____

_____

Looking back over time, how has your style served you well? How has it limited your effectiveness? Why?

_____

_____

_____

What are the behaviors and characteristics of the people you most enjoy? Why do you like being with them? Is there a pattern among these people?

_____

_____

_____

What are the behaviors and characteristics of the people you avoid? Why do you avoid them? Is there a pattern among these people?

_____

_____

_____

How do you think your behavioral style has affected your job and work culture choices? Has it played a role? Why?

_____

_____

_____

The High D:
"Give me a challenge and get out of the way!"

Introduction

In this chapter, you will get an in-depth view of people who have the High D, Dominance, tendency or style. These kinds of people thrive on producing results by controlling their environment. We will cover the subtleties of what motivates and demotivates them and how they typically affect others. Next, you will discover specific jobs (and cultures) that are a good match for High Ds, and we will cover the jobs and situations that would be demotivating for High Ds.

Review of the Dominance Style

In High Ds you will see behavior characterized by self-confidence, decisiveness, and risk-taking. They have a preference to detach from others and exert control over the people and circumstances of their lives. People with a high level of the D behavioral style demonstrate many interrelated strengths. They tend to

- accept challenges
- focus on producing concrete results
- be highly self-motivated
- enjoy solving problems
- decide quickly, even in the absence of abundant data
- challenge the status quo.

However, most Ds show a range of limiting behaviors that can hinder their effectiveness. If they do not manage themselves well, they can tend to

- be impatient with people and events
- show—at least on the surface—a lack of concern for others
- be overly blunt in their communications
- be high-strung, and not relaxed
- react strongly to the efforts of others to challenge or control them.

Variations on the D Theme: Four Different Behavior Patterns

We know from research that many people (around 75 percent) typically have a blend of two, sometimes even three, behavioral tendencies that show up in their behavioral patterns. The remaining 25 percent tend to show only one tendency. I call the singularly high patterns—those with only one high tendency—the pure styles.

This issue of behavioral blend is very significant when it comes to understanding yourself, understanding others, and picking the right job or place to work. This is because, given the High D behavior grouping, a person with a certain behavioral blend may be a natural for one job and may not be a good fit for another. For example, if your behavior pattern is a High D-I, you would be a natural fit for a fast-paced sales or sales management job if that were what you wanted to do. However, with that style, you would probably experience considerable stress if you were to serve in the job of an accounting manager. Someone with a High D-C behavior pattern would feel much more at home in that job because of his or her deliberate, accurate, and forceful manner.

There are four main behavioral patterns, or blends, in the Dominance, or D group. As you read the brief descriptions of each, note the shape of the graph and the intensity (the higher the plot point, the more noticeable that behavior) of each of the behavioral tendencies.

People with the **Developer Pattern** thrive on new opportunities. They take responsibility for getting things done and seek new or innovative problem solving methods. They do best in environments where there is a chance to achieve their goals and where there is an opportunity for advancement and challenge.

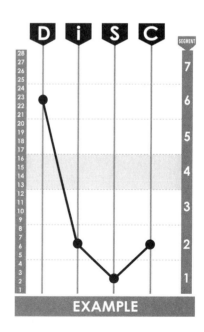

Developer

© 2001 by Inscape Publishing, Inc. All rights reserved. DiSC is a registered trademark of Inscape Publishing, Inc. •

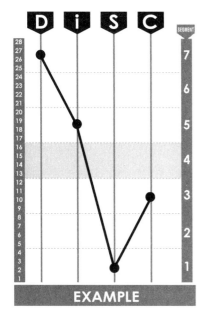

Result-Oriented

Those with a **Result-Oriented Pattern** work best when they can be both dominant and independent. They tend to seek environments that appreciate their persistence and doggedness. They do best in environments where there is an opportunity to test and develop their abilities to accomplish results.

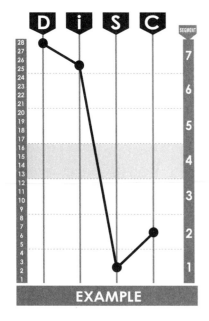

Inspirational

People with an **Inspirational Pattern** thrive in places where they can control their environment or audience. They tend to seek situations where they can act as people movers—initiating, demanding, complimenting, and disciplining. They do best in jobs and environments where they can accomplish goals through cooperation and persuasion, not overt domination.

People with the **Creative Pattern** do best in environments where they can be dominant and contribute unique accomplishments. They prefer situations where they can design or initiate change. They do best in jobs where they have the freedom to explore and the authority to examine and test their findings through action.

High D Behavioral Pattern People at Work: Some Real-Life Scenarios

Creative

Over the years, in both my personal and professional life, I have been a student of behavioral style. I have identified people's styles and observed them in the classroom, at work, and in my social and personal life. One thing seemed clear to me: Personal behavioral style is a key determinant in how we approach our lives and our work and in how successful and happy we are in given situations. This fact led me to conduct some practical research. I wanted to find out from real people of each of the DiSC® patterns what they would say about the kind of work that interests them and what is motivating and demotivating to them.

Therefore, I surveyed and interviewed several people in each of the four behavioral domains. I first asked them to name a job from their career in which they were most satisfied and productive. Then I asked them to select from a list of 32 behaviors (eight of each style) the top six behaviors they tended to use most often in that job. I asked them to describe how they approached their work, what motivated them at work, and what demotivated them. I selected four people from each of the behavioral domains (D, I, S, and C) and wrote brief scenarios for each. Their stories are interesting and unique.

© 2001 by Inscape Publishing, Inc. All rights reserved. DiSC is a registered trademark of Inscape Publishing, Inc.

I hope that they help you to see how style influences people's behavior and how style could influence your motivation or demotivation at work. When you read the scenarios, put yourself into them, and ask yourself the following:

- If I were in this job, would I approach it in the same way? Why? Why not?
- Would the same things motivate me? Why? Why not?
- Would the same things demotivate me? Why? Why not?
- Do I know anyone like this? If so, who? What kind of work do they do?

By answering these questions, you will begin to understand your own behaviors and motives and make important connections about the kind of work you do now, or might enjoy doing, and how you do or would approach your work.

Warren—Developer Pattern (Pure High D)

Warren is the senior human resources executive in a large, growing construction company. He is responsible for all the programs and staff normally associated with the human resources function, e.g., staffing, training, employee relations, and performance systems. Warren came to the organization when the human resources function was in its infancy. Over several years, he has built a strong team and many valuable programs in support of the company's human resources requirements.

It is no wonder that Warren named this job as his most satisfying and productive because as a Developer, he could not ask for a better situation to take on challenges and build things of importance. Warren is skilled at establishing vision, setting clear goals, acquiring the right resources, and getting things done. He is quite versatile and accommodating of others, but if things get off track, Warren's High D will not let things stray too long before setting it straight. He is a producer.

 © 2001 by Inscape Publishing, Inc. All rights reserved. DiSC is a registered trademark of Inscape Publishing, Inc.

Warren cited several behaviors that he routinely uses to be effective in his job. They align closely with someone of his DiSC® pattern. He uses the following behaviors most frequently:

- identifies problems, subjects, or priorities to be addressed
- takes initiative to start long- or short-term projects
- seeks and evaluates information before making decisions
- cites evidence to support a decision
- persuades others to his point of view
- encourages the personal efforts of others.

When asked about the greatest motivators in this job, his answers came as no surprise. Those that he mentioned align quite closely with someone of Warren's High D Developer pattern. He cited the most motivational aspects of his job as

- planning and creating direction for his team because this is one of his personal strengths
- building a team because the right people build the capability needed to get results
- influencing the company's leaders because in doing so he can have an effect on things that matter
- producing results, because it is so fulfilling.

The biggest demotivators in Warren's job stem from his need to produce results and his need to contribute to the company's performance. Most demotivating to Warren is

- micro-management by senior leaders because it is not needed and it erodes trust and confidence
- delayed decisions because they result in wasted time, rework, and schedule compression needed to catch up
- lack of recognition because it is a potential sign from his leaders of the lack of perceived value in what he is contributing (Note: High Is might cite the same demotivator, but the

© 2001 by Inscape Publishing, Inc. All rights reserved. DiSC is a registered trademark of Inscape Publishing, Inc.

reasoning would be different—they would most likely see it as a sign of personal rejection rather than not producing useful results.)

- lack of regular inclusion at top management meetings because this could be a potential sign of the unimportance of his role or low confidence in his contributions.

As you read Warren's scenario, did you find his motivators and demotivators similar to yours? If not, how are they different? Can you see yourself performing your work in a similar way?

John—Result-Oriented Pattern (High D, moderately High I)

John is a recently retired director of vocational education who had total responsibility for managing a large number of vocational programs, services, and staff in a large suburban school district. John is a hard charger who was at the forefront of his profession for years. He was highly respected by his peers for his leadership, innovations, and ability to run high-quality programs. He is skilled at forming good working relationships and is quite versatile in his behavior. John is least versatile when others attempt to take advantage of him or try to control things in his area of responsibility.

Predictably, when asked what behaviors he most frequently used, John mentioned things that are the stock-in-trade for someone of his High D-I, Result-Oriented pattern. High on his list were
- problem solving and priority setting
- facilitating interaction with others to get things done
- seeking new ideas and methods
- persuading others to his point of view
- taking initiative to start projects
- resolving differences with others through discussion.

42 • © 2001 by Inscape Publishing, Inc. All rights reserved. DiSC is a registered trademark of Inscape Publishing, Inc.

The biggest motivators in John's director job were what we would expect from someone with a High D-I behavior pattern:

- He liked challenges and problem solving because they helped him achieve his goals.
- He liked fighting the odds and creating strategies to win because it gave him a sense of victory and helped him prevail in spite of difficulties.
- He liked moving people toward excellence and figuring out the underlying motives necessary to succeed because this involved skillful maneuvering.
- He liked new problems and threats because he enjoyed confronting people and solving issues.
- He liked the freedom to think and act because it supported his need for independence.
- He liked the power of his position and being able to control the money because he could make decisions and act on them.

When asked about the demotivators in his work, John's responses evolved around his need for control, independence, and decisiveness. Specifically, he cited

- he didn't like dictatorial leaders because they hold you back
- he was impatient with long meetings because they are boring and a waste of time
- situations where, because of restrictive duties, he could not exercise a full range of options that might have been more useful
- situations where personal agendas and organizational game-playing blocked productive work and sapped his time and energy.

As you read John's scenario, did you find his motivators and demotivators similar to yours? If not, how are they different? Can you see yourself performing your work in a similar way?

© 2001 by Inscape Publishing, Inc. All rights reserved. DiSC is a registered trademark of Inscape Publishing, Inc.

Judith—Inspirational Pattern (Nearly equaly High D and I)

Judith is the owner and head salesperson of a small insurance brokerage firm that serves many small-to-medium-sized businesses with employee insurance programs and services. She leads a team of 12 people in the mission of providing high-quality, personal insurance products and services at a fair price.

Judith started in the insurance business as a claims clerk and quickly found her way into sales in the firm where she worked. After about 10 years, she arranged with her employer to buy a book of business and launched her own company with customers she had developed.

In true Inspirational style, Judith never lets too much grass grow under her feet. She moves fast, decides quickly, enjoys others, and produces results. Because of her High I, she is usually quite persuasive, warm, and responsive with others. However, with her equally High D, Judith can be very dominant and assertive when things do not go the way she wants. You know when you have been sliced and diced by a strong D like her.

Judith cited several behaviors as important in her work as the head of her firm and its lead salesperson. The behaviors square up well with what we would expect from a High D-I Inspirational pattern:

- moving forcefully, even if some people are offended
- coping with frequent interruptions and change
- acting decisively in situations where her past experience does not apply
- facilitating interaction between people to achieve results
- using persistence to perform routine activities
- supplying information without showing an opinion.

Judith named several aspects of her work as highly motivating. They are

- meeting and interacting with people because she enjoys it a great deal
- conducting insurance plan reviews and making recommendations to her customers because she enjoys using her knowledge and skills to inform, persuade, and produce results
- working in a competitive environment because it makes her work harder
- giving good customer service because every day is different and it is satisfying to help people.

Again, the demotivators of Judith's job as owner and chief sales person of her own insurance brokerage firm were consistent with what you would expect to hear from someone with her High D-I behavior pattern. She is demotivated by

- performing tedious tasks such as detailed account planning because it can be quite boring
- assisting customers' employees and plan sponsors with information they already have because it is time consuming and repetitive and the customers often don't appreciate her efforts
- the stress of constantly reselling the same customers year after year because she cannot take anything for granted.

As you read Judith's scenario, did you find her motivators and demotivators similar to yours. If not, how are they different? Can you see yourself performing your work in a similar way?

Larry—Creative Pattern (Nearly equal High D and C)

Larry said his most satisfying job was as the commander of a systems-oriented division of a large urban police department. He is a 30-year

© 2001 by Inscape Publishing, Inc. All rights reserved. DiSC is a registered trademark of Inscape Publishing, Inc.

police veteran. He worked several years as a patrol officer. Then, through promotions to sergeant and lieutenant over the years, he worked his way up through several divisional assignments such as patrol, juvenile, vice, and research and development before assuming the division commander job.

In this job, Larry led a team of six sworn police officers and about the same number of civilian employees. He had many responsibilities including setting department policy, overseeing operations, budgeting, staffing, and performance management. His duties also included public and police relations, interagency law-enforcement coordination, selling and promoting his department services, and city council relations. It was a demanding, high-profile job.

Larry was so good at the job that he held it eight years longer than normal for such an assignment. He excelled at the work because of his drive, determination, multiple technical and police skills, and interpersonal skills. He was analytical, a thorough planner, and a great executor—all hallmarks of the High D-C style. He was also good at forming interpersonal relationships, but if things got too sloppy or if results were not happening, the charm dropped and his forceful, analytical persona took charge.

When asked what behaviors he used most often on the job, Larry replied with a list that is characteristic of a High D-C Creative pattern. He said he frequently
- coped with change and interruptions
- took the initiative to start large long-term projects
- enjoyed interacting with people who were different than him
- verbally encouraged others in their efforts
- interacted with new people

 © 2001 by Inscape Publishing, Inc. All rights reserved. DiSC is a registered trademark of Inscape Publishing, Inc.

- listened analytically
- questioned when necessary and cooperated with others to solve problems.

Larry derived much enjoyment from his work as a division commander. All of the motivators he cited fit with the types of things you would expect to hear from someone with his DiSC® pattern. The most motivational aspects of the job for Larry were

- the opportunity to initiate and direct change because this played well to his problem-solving instincts
- being proactive in enforcing the state laws and city ordinances because it assured compliance and things did not get out of control in his area of jurisdiction
- creating a completely new automated system for managing a large amount of data stemming from transactions that occurred in the community because it had true value and usefulness
- leading the department staff, especially the police officers, because it challenged his experience and knowledge of law enforcement and business.

The demotivators that Larry mentioned all related to his work ethic, expertise, and personal integrity—all matters of high importance to the typical High D-C individual. He cited as demotivators

- the heavy workload (much of it self-imposed) because it took its toll in high stress and in the feeling that he was failing in parts of his job
- the occasional personal attacks by business people affected by his enforcement efforts because the attacks challenged his professional and personal integrity and affected department morale
- the occasional attacks by politicians driven by their self-interests with no concern for facts or truth because it affected his and the department's morale and stifled initiative.

As you read Larry's scenario, did you find his motivators and demotivators similar to yours? If not, how are they different? Can you see yourself performing your work in a similar way?

Finding the Fit: Suitable Jobs for a High D

So, what are the career-fields, jobs, and workplaces that are most suitable for the High D? Clearly, like each of the other behavioral style groups, this style has many unique natural strengths and characteristics. They are strong-willed, independent, practical, decisive, and efficient. Because of this, High Ds would do well to seek jobs and work environments where they can

- thrive in positions of leadership because they like to be in charge and tell others what to do
- focus on tasks and produce results
- readily accept challenges and responsibility because it meets their need for action and control
- communicate clearly and directly about things
- exercise their power in getting things done
- take risks and participate in or lead change in an organization
- organize and structure things well to achieve efficiency in the workplace
- make quick decisions and control their outcomes
- be self-motivated and action-oriented
- compete and overcome opposition.

High Ds would most likely be least comfortable in jobs and work cultures where

- others try to micro manage their work
- people are too sensitive about things
- there is undue hesitation before deciding

- decisions are overanalyzed, i.e., analysis paralysis
- weakness is shown in the face of adversity.

Before you zero in on any particular job and make a choice, remember this key point: You can be satisfied and productive in any job, no matter your style. However, you must be prepared to adapt to the various roles required in your job. (See the in-depth discussion of role adaptation in Chapter 2.) This is important, because some jobs and roles may require more flexibility from you than you are prepared to give. That said, the following are some examples of careers and jobs most likely to be attractive for High Ds:

- executive, general manager
- police officer, investigator
- manufacturing manager
- military officer, enlisted person
- politician
- entrepreneur
- attorney
- medical doctor
- tax accountant
- realtor
- professional critic
- general contractor
- construction project manager, superintendent, or tradesperson
- sales/sales manager
- marketing manager
- clergyperson (in some settings)
- school superintendent, director.

The Link Between Your Pattern and Job or Culture Requirements

In reality, the connection between your behavior pattern and a job fit may not be as tight as you might think. Just because you are high in the dominance tendency does not necessarily mean that you will be very happy and effective being in charge in any organization. This is because organizations have different needs and cultures. For example, if you were a clergyperson with a High Dominance-Influence style, you would feel very much at home and needed in a congregation that is just starting up or in a rebuilding mode. However, if you were a clergyperson with High Steadiness-Conscientiousness behavior pattern, you would probably be more comfortable and welcome in a smaller, more stable congregation populated with multi-generational families. Another example of this would be a situation where, as a High Dominance-Conscientiousness attorney, you might choose to be the head lawyer in the formal environment of a corporate law department. Conversely, if you had a High Influence-Steadiness pattern you might be happier and more effective in a low-key, friendly family-law practice.

Given your style, if you choose a work culture that fits your emotional needs, you will likely be in a position to satisfy those needs, and there is good chance that you will be effective in your work. My personal story, outlined in the preface, in which I changed jobs as an unfulfilled High I, in a High C culture, to a hugging in the hallways kind of culture, attests to this.

 © 2001 by Inscape Publishing, Inc. All rights reserved. DiSC is a registered trademark of Inscape Publishing, Inc.

Chapter Summary

As we have seen, those with a High D behavior pattern are results focused, action oriented, and straight talking. They do well in jobs and work environments where they have a high degree of independence, authority, and accountability. Beyond this, there is another aspect of behavioral style that could influence the kind of specific job or work culture you should choose. Depending on their specific DiSC® classical pattern, i.e., Creative, Inspirational, Developer, or Result-Oriented, a person might be particularly well suited for one job and culture, but have to adjust extensively for another. Finally, if you are able to be in work and a work culture that is a reasonably good fit, there is a good chance that you will be happier and more productive.

© 2001 by Inscape Publishing, Inc. All rights reserved. DiSC is a registered trademark of Inscape Publishing, Inc.

Some Things to Think About

As you read the scenarios of the High D people in this chapter, did you see any similarities between you and them? If so, what did you see that seemed true for you? If not, what was different for you?

_____

_____

_____

_____

What jobs, past or present, have you had where you experienced similar style-related motivators? How did they affect your job satisfaction and effectiveness?

_____

_____

_____

_____

What jobs, past or present, have you had where there were far more style-related demotivators than there were motivators? How did this affect your job satisfaction and effectiveness?

_____

_____

_____

_____

If you are a High D and searching for a good fit job or career field, what kinds of work do you think would be a good fit for you, assuming you were otherwise fully qualified? If not fully qualified, what would it take for you to be so?

_____

_____

_____

_____

If you are a High D and in a job that is not a good fit, how can you adapt (see Chapter 7) or change things to make it a better fit?

_____

_____

_____

_____

The High I:
"No matter what, I've got to work with people who are enthusiastic and interactive!"

Introduction

In this chapter we will focus in depth on people who have the High I, Influence, tendency or style. These people thrive in situations where they can shape their world by persuading and influencing others. In learning more about the High I, we will discuss the things that motivate and demotivate them in the workplace, and how they typically affect others. Given this background, you will discover specific jobs and cultures that are a good fit for High Is, and we will cover jobs and situations that would be demotivating for them.

Review of the Influence Style

In the High I, Influence, style you will notice behavior characterized by enthusiasm, charm, and sociability. They have a preference to affiliate with others and to exert control over the people and the circumstances that affect them. People with a high amount of this tendency display many interrelated strengths. They tend to

- generate enthusiasm in others around them
- view people and situations optimistically
- initiate relationships with others
- participate effectively in group situations
- move rather quickly with high energy
- readily verbalize issues and concepts.

As with other styles, High Is show a range of limiting behaviors as well, any one of which could hinder their effectiveness. If not self-managed well, they tend to

- be overly expressive, i.e., they can talk too much
- be overly concerned about the feelings of others
- show impatience with details and complexity
- make sweeping generalizations and exaggerate
- make impulsive, emotionally based decisions
- not focus strongly on results, but more on relationships.

Variations on the I Theme: Four Behavior Patterns

In chapter 3, we discussed how most of us display a behavioral blend of two or more tendencies, whereas only about 25 percent have only one dominant tendency. As we know, our behavioral blend is vitally important when it comes to job satisfaction and effectiveness. For example, if you were a High I-C behavior pattern you would likely feel comfortable in a job requiring good relationship and organization skills, such as a personnel recruiter or customer service representative. Alternatively, as a High I-S you would likely be comfortable and effective as a teacher, counselor, or retail salesperson. However, as a pure High I, what if you wound up in a job where you were isolated from others? The answer is obvious: You would probably soon be out creating conversations and relationships and might forget what you were actually hired for.

There are four main behavioral patterns, or blends, in the Influence family. As you read the brief descriptions of each, note the shape of the graph and the intensity (the higher the plot point, the more noticeable that behavior) of each of the behavioral tendencies.

Those with a **Promoter pattern** thrive in situations where they can develop and maintain friendships. They tend to participate and interact well with others in activities and may be less interested in task accomplishment. They tend to do best in jobs where they are able to relieve tension and promote projects and people, including themselves.

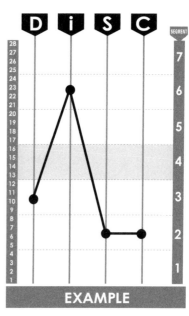

Promoter

© 2001 by Inscape Publishing, Inc. All rights reserved. DiSC is a registered trademark of Inscape Publishing, Inc. •

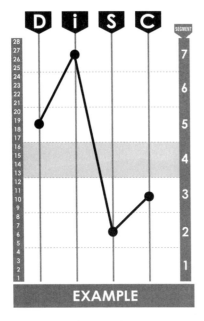

Persuader

People with the **Persuader pattern** work best in situations where they can work with others, receive challenging assignments, and experience a variety of work activities that require mobility. They tend to be friendly, open with their feelings, direct, and verbally adept. They tend to do best in jobs that require selling, closing, and delegating responsibility.

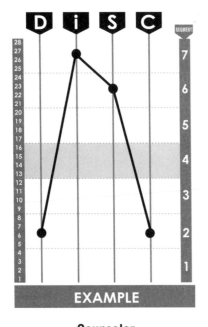

Counselor

People with the **Counselor pattern** flourish in places where they can be involved in solving people problems. They tend to be optimistic, warm, empathetic, and understanding. Counselors tend to do well in work that involves meeting the needs of people, rather than strict task accomplishment.

 © 2001 by Inscape Publishing, Inc. All rights reserved. DiSC is a registered trademark of Inscape Publishing, Inc.

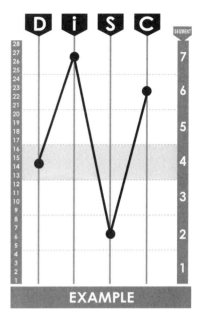

Appraiser

Those with the **Appraiser pattern** thrive in environments where they can accomplish goals through teamwork. They are typically persuasive, organized, competitive, and assertive. They do well in jobs where they can exert their positive, cooperative approach to accomplish job goals and activities with others.

High I Behavioral Pattern People at Work: Some Real-Life Scenarios

As you recall from Chapter 3, I did some practical research with people about what motivated or demotivated them in a job where they were both satisfied and effective. I then summarized their situations in scenarios designed to help you gain a view of what it is like for people of certain styles to work in various jobs. This information can be enormously valuable as you consider your own job needs.

When you read the scenarios, put yourself into them, and ask yourself the following questions:

- If I were in this job, would I approach it in the same way? Why? Why not?
- Would the same things motivate me? Why? Why not?
- Would the same things demotivate me? Why? Why not?
- Do I know anyone like this? If so, who? What kind of work do they do?

© 2001 by Inscape Publishing, Inc. All rights reserved. DiSC is a registered trademark of Inscape Publishing, Inc.

By answering the questions, you will begin to understand your own behaviors and motives and make important connections about the kind of work you do now, or might enjoy doing, and how you do, or would, approach your work.

Phillip—Promoter Pattern (Pure High I)

Phillip reports his favorite job to be that of a hotel bellman in a large downtown hotel. He is responsible for meeting and greeting guests, assisting with their luggage, showing them to their rooms, running errands, and providing other services, as required, that make the guests' stay as comfortable as possible.

Phillip started with the hotel as a part-timer during his first year of community college and continued full time after he graduated with an associate's degree in general business. He has been doing this job for over 10 years. This kind of work fits well with Phillip's style because he is friendly and strives to make people feel welcome. In addition, he doesn't have to mess with any details or paperwork, which suits him just fine. Phillip meets many new customers each day, as well as the hotel's regular customers who return repeatedly. For outstanding work and personal service, he gets plenty of recognition in the form of personal praise and tips. He has also been Employee of the Quarter many times and Employee of the Year twice.

Phillip cited several behaviors he routinely uses to be most effective in his job. They closely align with what you would expect to see in someone with his pure High I pattern. He most frequently

- responds to the needs and feelings of his customers
- displays restraint when feeling anxious or impatient
- interacts with a variety of people

• © 2001 by Inscape Publishing, Inc. All rights reserved. DiSC is a registered trademark of Inscape Publishing, Inc.

- interacts frequently with new people
- is optimistic in responding to people's concerns and needs
- works cooperatively with others on the team to serve the hotel's customers well.

When asked about the greatest motivators of his job, Phillip's answers were very consistent with what one might expect from a High I Promoter pattern. He cites the most motivational aspects of his job as

- meeting and greeting people all day long because he loves being with people and serving their needs
- being up, showing his customers and others that he is enjoying their company
- conversing with customers about their needs and concerns because it gives him a chance to talk and solve problems. (Note: Phillip said that, in each case, he has to read the customer to judge whether that person wants to talk or just go to his room quietly. Phillip knows his style can be wearing to some people, so he has to watch it.)
- enjoying constant variety and activity because it hardly ever gets boring
- being onstage, in uniform, serving people because it gives him visibility and recognition.

Most demotivating to Phillip are
- slow periods at certain times of the day because it can be boring
- unfriendly, stuffy customers because he doesn't really know if they are angry with him or at something else
- squabbles amongst the hotel bell staff, sometimes over petty issues, because people ought to be more positive and make an effort to get along

© 2001 by Inscape Publishing, Inc. All rights reserved. DiSC is a registered trademark of Inscape Publishing, Inc.

- people who don't seem to appreciate his efforts because he wants to do his best and to be recognized.

As you read Phillip's scenario, did you find his motivators and demotivators similar to yours? If not, how are they different? Can you see yourself performing your work in a similar way?

Rick—Persuader Pattern (High I, Moderate D)

Rick was most effective and satisfied in a previous job as a national sales manager for a manufacturer of aftermarket automotive parts. In this job, he led a team of 15 sales people and customer service representatives to meet customer needs and achieve his company's sales targets. He was responsible for recruiting and hiring staff, coaching and training sales people, market planning, administering the sales budget, coordinating big deals, and serving on the company's senior leadership team.

Rick worked his way up to sales management over a period of 15 years, during which time he sold in several markets. He knew his markets, customers, and products well. Rick was skilled at getting the best out of his people. He earned their respect and willingness to perform by being open, reliable, accepting, and consistent. Rick had strong emotional control and was able to adjust to different circumstances and keep his cool under fire. This kind of adaptability served him well in his role.

Rick cited several key behaviors that he used most frequently in his sales manager job. They are entirely consistent with those of a High I-D Persuader pattern. He used these behaviors most frequently:

- moved forcefully at times, even if some were offended
- interacted frequently with new people
- sought new ideas and methods for achieving results
- facilitated interaction between people to get results

 • © 2001 by Inscape Publishing, Inc. All rights reserved. DiSC is a registered trademark of Inscape Publishing, Inc.

- took initiative to start large or long-term projects
- sought and evaluated information before making decisions
- verbally encouraged others in their personal efforts.

Given Rick's style, his greatest motivators on the job were what you would expect. They were

- acting in a leadership role because he was able to influence people to produce positive performance and results
- achieving measurable results because it gave him immediate feedback and reinforcement for his work
- being a reasonable boss because his people were then able to express their ideas, opinions, and suggestions without fear
- selling his ideas and positions to the senior team because he was able to get the tools and resources he needed to run an effective sales organization.

Rick's biggest demotivators are typical for someone with his pattern, especially working in a sales environment. Most demotivating to Rick were

- constant travel because it required time away from home and family
- the inability to influence customers to move away from a competitive offer because if he couldn't persuade them it meant lost sales
- unnecessary paperwork because it often did not add much value to reaching the sales goals
- constant pressure to attain sales goals because even if you are on target for the current quarter, there is always next quarter.

As you read Rick's scenario, did you find his motivators and demotivators similar to yours? If not, how are they different? Can you see yourself performing your work in a similar way?

© 2001 by Inscape Publishing, Inc. All rights reserved. DiSC is a registered trademark of Inscape Publishing, Inc. • 63

Rachel—Counselor Pattern (High I, Moderate S)

Rachel's most satisfying job was that of a training coordinator in a large insurance company. She started in this job after graduating with a degree in human resources management. She was in this job for three years and consistently performed it in an outstanding manner. Because of this, Rachel recently earned a promotion to the job of personnel recruiter. She enjoys the new job as well, mainly for the chance to visit college campuses and meet new prospective employees and sell them on the opportunities at her company.

As training coordinator, Rachel had a variety of duties. She supported senior trainers by coordinating learning materials, doing class set-ups, and assisting in the facilitation of some classes.

Her main job, and the most satisfying to her, was to coordinate and conduct the monthly new-employee orientation program. In this role, she scheduled participants, lined up speakers, assured a high-quality program, and supported the new employees. Over the three-day orientation program, she developed a personal connection with each new employee. Rachel also worked with the new employees' supervisors to make certain that new employees felt welcome and confident about their new beginnings in the company. She maintained personal contact with them throughout the extended orientation period (one month). Rachel was, in effect, the guarantee tag to ensure that all went well for the newcomers in their first month of their employment with the company.

Rachel has had a variety of jobs during school and after college, but so far, the training coordinator job is her favorite. This is because she was able to do things that were pleasing to her. She said the behaviors she most frequently used in the job were

- interacting with new people

 • © 2001 by Inscape Publishing, Inc. All rights reserved. DiSC is a registered trademark of Inscape Publishing, Inc.

- working cooperatively with others to complete tasks
- interacting with people who had different styles
- listening analytically, questioning when necessary
- coping with interruptions and change
- showing understanding by responding to the feelings of others
- verbally encouraging others in their personal efforts.

These behaviors are very consistent with someone of Rachel's High I-S Counselor pattern.

When asked about the most motivating aspects of her job, Rachel's answers came as no great surprise when you consider the people orientation of those with a High I-S Counselor behavior pattern. She said the most motivating aspects of her job were

- constantly meeting new people because it gave her a chance to build new friendships in the company
- supporting new employees because it gave her an outlet to be in contact and to listen to and follow through on issues that were important to them
- being in a visible role because she enjoyed that kind of exposure
- working with her internal customers, both employees and supervisors, because it allowed her to help them solve problems and get the answers they needed
- not being reactive, but working in a stable and predictable way, because others knew they could rely on her when they needed help.

Rachel cited the most demotivating aspects of her job as a training coordinator were

- tension that inevitably came up between supervisors and her when she had to get them to follow through on their

© 2001 by Inscape Publishing, Inc. All rights reserved. DiSC is a registered trademark of Inscape Publishing, Inc.

orientation tasks because she didn't like to make demands and upset others

- program administrative tasks because she is not particularly detail-oriented and she had to really stretch to do this well
- constant pressure and demands to plan and manage her calendar well because she would rather just take things as they come and help people with their needs
- the negative people she had to deal with because she believes that life is better when you can see the positive side of things.

As you read Rachel's scenario, did you find her motivators and demotivators similar to yours? If not, how are they different? Can you see yourself performing your work in a similar way?

Brenda—Appraiser Pattern (High I, Moderate C)

Brenda is most satisfied and effective in her present job as a production team leader in a manufacturing company. Her company produces a line of glass products used by original equipment manufacturers.

Through her people, Brenda is responsible for meeting unit production, quality, and financial goals. Her main duties consist of staff selection, training, scheduling, performance planning and feedback, safety, production planning, monitoring production and quality, and coordinating machine maintenance and repair. She is also a member of the company's senior manufacturing team, a group of senior production people who plan and implement overall plant production improvements.

Brenda joined the company eight years ago, after attending a few quarters of college. She was not a motivated student at the time. A few years ago, she began attending night classes and is close to getting an associate degree in manufacturing.

• © 2001 by Inscape Publishing, Inc. All rights reserved. DiSC is a registered trademark of Inscape Publishing, Inc.

Her first job at the company was as a line feeder operator, placing raw materials on the line at the beginning of the manufacturing process. From there she became a cutter operator, a more highly skilled position where mistakes could result in very costly scrap. After four years with the company, she became a production quality coordinator. Then, because of her excellent work, job experiences, and education attainment, she was a natural for the team leader job.

As a High I-C pattern, Brenda refers to herself as a person of opposites. She can be charming and very people-oriented, but when things get a little messy and do not meet her high performance standards, she can be quite "nasty and persnickety" (her words).

Brenda says that, for her, this type of work is like being a duck in water. In the production environment she uses her High I-C strengths to the best advantage. When asked what behaviors she uses most, she said she

- verbally encourages others in their personal efforts
- identifies problems, subjects, or priorities
- chooses carefully among alternatives before acting
- persuades others to her point of view
- listens analytically, questioning when necessary
- monitors and maintains key requirements for quality or safety
- facilitates interaction between people to achieve results.

When asked, Brenda recalled many motivators in her job as production team leader. Most of them are very consistent with someone of her High I-C Appraiser behavior pattern:

- consistently achieving the production goals because she is competitive and wants to succeed
- working as a team to accomplish goals because it involves people and planning, two of her favorite things

© 2001 by Inscape Publishing, Inc. All rights reserved. DiSC is a registered trademark of Inscape Publishing, Inc.

- having a high-performing production team because it is a reward for all their training and hard work
- dealing with production problems and issues because it gives her a chance to be creative and get others involved
- serving on the senior production process team because it is a chance to be creative and make a long-term difference in their plant's productivity.

Brenda cited several things about her job that are demotivating. As you read them, try to see if you can see the connection between these demotivators and her High I-C behavior pattern:

- people who are slow to react to situations or avoid initiating actions to fix things because she believes that if they sit around too long nothing will ever get done
- people who cannot take her verbal feedback because unless they talk about issues they will never improve
- the lack of routine positive feedback from her boss because they are doing well and she thinks she should be recognized more for her efforts
- the sometimes boring routine of manufacturing because she likes excitement and the chance to do new things.

As you read Brenda's scenario, did you find her motivators and demotivators similar to yours? If not, how are they different? Can you see yourself performing your work in a similar way?

Finding the Fit: Suitable Jobs for a High I

So, what career fields, jobs, or workplaces are most suitable for the High I? As we know, they thrive in situations where they can shape their world by persuading and influencing others. They bring many good qualities to the table. High Is are ambitious, stimulating, enthusiastic, dramatic, and friendly. In choosing career fields, jobs, and work environments, they should be where they can

- relate to others in a friendly, approachable manner
- apply their optimistic, enthusiastic approach to opportunities and problems
- motivate and influence others through their persuasiveness and openly verbalize their thoughts and feelings
- work toward known, specific, and quickly attainable objectives, rather than long, drawn-out work
- be involved on the start-up of projects and initiatives and let others carry out the work
- work in stimulating environments that are friendly, informal, and favorable
- get immediate favorable feedback on their accomplishments and work when warranted
- lead or participate in groups and build alliances to get results
- perform in situations free of strong controls, details, or complexity.

High Is would most likely be least comfortable in work cultures and jobs where

- people are not recognized for their contributions
- rules dominate over common sense
- people are too cautious
- analysis is favored over action
- feelings are ignored
- people are quiet and introverted.

As we have discussed, you can be successful in any job, regardless of your behavioral style, if you adapt to the role requirements of your job. However, we also know that it makes good sense to get into a job that is a good fit at the outset because some jobs and roles may require more flexibility from you than you are prepared to give. That said, the following are some examples of careers and jobs most likely to be attractive for High Is:

- trainer/facilitator
- consultant
- travel agent
- theme park worker
- flight attendant
- restaurant server or host
- recreation leader
- hair stylist
- entertainer
- radio/TV broadcaster, reporter
- tour guide
- insurance agent
- help-desk attendant
- receptionist
- salesperson
- customer service (especially when combined with "inside sales")
- retail worker
- clergyperson
- advertising agent
- public relations specialist
- actor, musician
- employment recruiter
- politician.

The Link Between Your Pattern and Job or Culture Requirements

We know from previous chapters that just finding any job or organization doesn't necessarily mean you will be a good fit if the culture isn't a good fit. For example, if you were an outgoing, friendly, expressive, and action-oriented High I-D person, you would likely feel completely out of place in an organizational culture that values deliberateness, formality, and low-key communications. This is critical for you to consider because just as you have your needs and preferences, organizations have theirs.

As I wrote in the introduction, given my High I-D behavior pattern, I was extremely unhappy in a company that valued accuracy, completeness, and emotional reserve. I accepted that to a point, but after three years of constant adaptation, I depleted my emotional energy. Upon accepting a new job in a company where they valued creativity, enthusiasm, and optimism, I felt happy and satisfied within a few weeks. The culture and I were a match!

Another example of the importance of fit would be the job of opening a new sales territory. This would involve making many new contacts, experiencing turndowns and rejection, and doing a great deal of pioneering work. It would likely be a natural fit for people with a High I-D Persuader pattern because of their energy, enthusiasm, and persuasiveness. However, the job would likely be very stressful for people with a High I-S Counselor pattern because they like close, personal relationships and would likely shudder at the cold calling and rejections inherent in such work. Someone of the Counselor pattern might feel more comfortable and be more productive in a sales support or inside sales job.

Chapter Summary

People with a High I behavior pattern tend to be people-oriented, optimistic, and enthusiastic. They thrive in job and work culture situations where they can relate to others in a friendly manner, apply their enthusiastic, optimistic approach to working and solving problems, and motivate and influence others through their persuasiveness. One's unique High I DiSC® behavioral pattern, i.e., Promoter, Persuader, Counselor, or Appraiser, should play a key role in the specific kind of work or work culture one chooses. This is because some jobs might be entirely appropriate for one pattern, but not another. For example, a person with an Inspirational pattern would be a natural as a sales manager. However, for someone with a Counselor pattern, some of the roles of a sales manager would require lots of stretching and redirecting. Ultimately, as we know, finding the right fit between your style and your job and work culture is one thing that will make you happier and more productive.

 © 2001 by Inscape Publishing, Inc. All rights reserved. DiSC is a registered trademark of Inscape Publishing, Inc.

Some Things to Think About

As you read the scenarios of the High I people in this chapter, did you see any similarity between you and them? If so, what did you see that seemed true for you? If not, what was different for you?

_____

_____

_____

_____

What jobs, past or present, have you had where you experienced similar style-related motivators? How did they affect your job satisfaction and effectiveness?

_____

_____

_____

_____

What jobs, past or present, have you had where there were far more style-related demotivators than there were motivators? How did this affect your job satisfaction and effectiveness?

_____

_____

_____

_____

If you are a High I and searching for a good fit job or career field, what kinds of work do you think would be a good fit for you, assuming you were otherwise fully qualified? If not fully qualified, what would it take for you to be so?

_____

_____

_____

_____

If you are a High I and in a job that is not a good fit, how can you adapt (see chapter 7) or change things to make it a better fit?

_____

_____

_____

_____

The High S:
"Let's work together and get this done in a calm and effective manner!"

Introduction

In this chapter, you will learn more about people who have the High S, Steadiness, tendency or style. High Ss thrive in situations where they can achieve stability and accomplish tasks by cooperating with others. We will cover the subtleties of what motivates and demotivates them and how they typically affect others in the work environment. We will then cover the specific jobs and kinds of work cultures that would be most motivating for High Ss, and we will cover the kinds of situations and jobs that would be demotivating for them.

Review of the Steadiness Style

When you observe the typical High S, you will see behavior characterized by patience, teamwork, stability, a methodical approach to things,
and calmness. They have a preference to affiliate with others and adapt
to the people and circumstances in their lives. Those with a high level
of steadiness behavior show many interrelated strengths. In general,
they tend to

- be dependable, loyal team workers
- be consistent in performing their work
- enjoy helping others
- be patient with people and situations
- create stable, harmonious work environments
- be good listeners—interested and empathetic.

High Ss can also show a range of limiting behaviors that can hinder
their effectiveness. If not self-managed well, they tend to

- be overly willing to give in to others, even to their own
  detriment
- resist positive change in order to maintain stability and
  predictability
- fear speaking out on issues, even when they have knowledge
  or an opinion about something being discussed
- be overly kind and tolerant
- procrastinate.

Variations on the S Theme:
Four Different Behavior Patterns

We know from previous sections of the book that, in general, about 75 percent of us display a blend of at least two prominent behavioral tendencies. Only about 25 percent of us have only one dominant tendency.

As we know, your style mix makes a big difference in the kind of job and work culture needed to make you most happy and productive. For example, if you had a High S-C behavior pattern you would make a perfect addition to a small team of coworkers. However, if you were a High S-D behavior pattern, unless you were mindful of and controlled your dominant tendencies, you could be a source of tension for your High S coworkers and experience tension yourself within the culture that such a mix of styles would produce. Such a scenario might go like this: "Can't we just get along? Why does he always have to go at it alone?"

There are actually four High S behavior patterns, or blends, in the Steadiness group. As you read the brief descriptions of each, note the shape of the graph and the intensity (the higher the plot point, the more noticeable that behavior) of each of the behavioral tendencies.

People with the **Specialist pattern** thrive in situations where they can perform short-term tasks in a steady, predictable, and consistent manner. They tend to work well with others because of their moderate, controlled approach and modest disposition. They tend to do best in specialized areas where they can do their work along directed channels and achieve consistent performance.

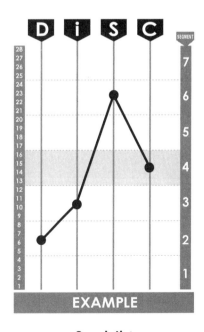

Specialist

© 2001 by Inscape Publishing, Inc. All rights reserved. DiSC is a registered trademark of Inscape Publishing, Inc.

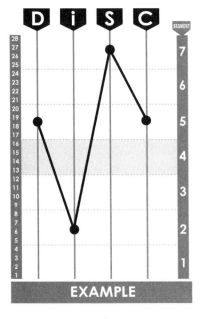

Investigator

People of the **Investigator pattern** are quite scarce in the general population (about 1.5 percent) because they have three high tendencies—S, D, and C. They tend to be dispassionate anchors of reality, calmly and steadily pursuing an independent path toward a fixed goal. They thrive best in challenging technical assignments in which they can use actual data to interpret information, draw conclusions, and work doggedly to accomplish tasks.

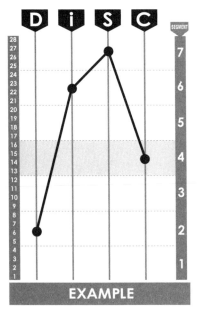

Agent

Those with the **Agent pattern** thrive in situations where they can offer friendship and service to others. They are great at attending to both the human relations and task aspects of their work. Agents make people feel wanted and needed. Because of their harmonious, friendly approach, they are particularly good at doing things for others that they would find difficult to do for themselves.

 © 2001 by Inscape Publishing, Inc. All rights reserved. DiSC is a registered trademark of Inscape Publishing, Inc.

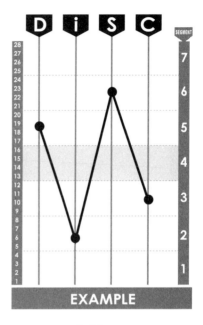

Achiever

People of the **Achiever pattern** are industrious and diligent in the performance of their work. They tend to be committed to their own goals rather than automatically accepting the broader goals of the organization. As a result, they develop a strong sense of accountability for their own performance. Achievers thrive in places where they can operate at peak efficiency and reap the rewards and recognition equal to their contribution.

High S Behavioral Pattern People at Work: Some Real-Life Scenarios

As you have read, in researching this book, I consulted with several people to see what motivated or demotivated them in a job where they were both satisfied and effective. Their scenarios, described below, will help you gain a view of what it is like for people of certain styles to work in various jobs. This information can be enormously valuable as you consider your own job needs. When you read the scenarios, I hope you will put yourself into the stories, and ask yourself the following:

- If I were in this job, would I approach it in the same way? Why? Why not?
- Would the same things motivate me? Why? Why not?
- Would the same things demotivate me? Why? Why not?
- Do I know anyone like this? If so, who? What kind of work do they do?

© 2001 by Inscape Publishing, Inc. All rights reserved. DiSC is a registered trademark of Inscape Publishing, Inc.

By answering these questions you will begin to understand your own behaviors and motives and make important connections about the kind of work you do now, or might enjoy doing, and how you do or would approach your work.

Pamela—Specialist Pattern (Pure High S)

Pamela, with a High S behavior pattern, cited her most productive and satisfying job was that of a medical office assistant working for a family practitioner in a small office. She started the job right out of high school and learned most of her medical office skills through on-the-job training. She also attended some medical assistant association training meetings from time to time. In high school, she had taken some basic clerical courses like keyboarding and accounting, which she found to be very helpful in the doctor's office. As a point of reference, Pamela's medical office work occurred in the early 1980s, a time when there were few computers, many single-doctor offices, and little regulation of medical office employees except for nurses and doctors. Today, to qualify for the same job, Pamela would have to be educated and certified as a medical office assistant.

Pamela had a wide variety of duties that, when done well, assured a smooth and well-run medical office. She and a coworker shared some duties, but they also had their own responsibilities. The doctor and two assistants worked well as a team and enjoyed their relationship.

Pamela's duties consisted of three main segments: patients, administration, and medical. In the area of patients, Pamela was responsible for greeting and making patients comfortable, conducting initial complaint screening interviews, bringing patients to the exam rooms, and introducing patients to the doctor if they were first-time patients. As a High S, Pamela cares deeply about people. Because of this, she always went the extra mile to make patients feel welcome and comfortable, especially the older ones. For many people, seeing a doctor, for any reason, can be stressful. Pamela's goal was to make things go a little easier for them.

Administratively, Pamela's main duties included pulling and refiling medical charts, transcribing the doctor's exam notes to the charts, billing patients, collecting payments, processing insurance claims, and maintaining the office's medical supplies. She also took care of the office laundry program (linens, uniforms, etc.). Since Pamela shows strong attention to detail, she was a stickler for accuracy and completeness when it came to administration—certainly a good quality in a medical office environment.

Pamela's main medical duties included assisting the doctor with basic physical exam tasks, such as weighing patients, taking blood pressure readings, administering blood, and doing urine tests. She also assisted the doctor in minor surgical procedures and administered various inoculations and booster shots. To assure clean space and tools, she also had to clean the medical spaces and sterilize all medical equipment and instruments.

Pamela cited several behaviors she routinely used to be most effective in her job. The behaviors closely align with what you would expect to see in someone with her High S pattern. She most frequently

- showed understanding of others by responding to their feelings
- followed detailed instructions step-by-step
- enjoyed interacting with people who had different styles
- performed repetitive tasks without losing motivation
- listened analytically, questioning when necessary
- received satisfaction from activities requiring predictable behavior.

© 2001 by Inscape Publishing, Inc. All rights reserved. DiSC is a registered trademark of Inscape Publishing, Inc.

When asked, Pamela recalled many motivators in her job as a medical office assistant. Most of them are very consistent with what you would expect from someone with her High S, Specialist, behavior pattern:

- seeing people get well because they were sick and her job was to help them
- making coffee and serving donuts to staff during breaks because she liked to serve others and enjoyed the informal breaks and conversation
- keeping busy with lots of activities because time went fast and it never got boring
- discovering and taking care of patient needs because she was able to serve them
- doing the office's bookkeeping because she enjoyed detailed work and making things balance
- keeping the office clean and replenishing the supplies because it contributed to a neat, tidy, and smoothly running office.

The demotivators of her position as a medical office assistant are consistent with what you would expect from someone with her High S Specialist behavior pattern:

- collecting past due accounts from patients, many of whom were poor or uninsured, because she did not like confronting people
- long, irregular hours on some days because she had other obligations and a family life that was important to her
- little or no approval for doing good work because it made her wonder if she was doing well enough
- the direct, impatient communication style of one of her doctor employers (in her second medical office job) because she was uncomfortable with that style of communication and it created fear in her.

 • © 2001 by Inscape Publishing, Inc. All rights reserved. DiSC is a registered trademark of Inscape Publishing, Inc.

As you read Pamela's scenario, did you find her motivators and demotivators similar to yours? If not, how are they different? Can you see yourself performing your work in a similar way?

Craig—Investigator Pattern (High S, High D, High C)

Craig has one of the rarer DiSC® patterns, held by only 1.5 percent of people in the general population. He named his current job of vice president of human resources in a small liberal arts college as his most productive and satisfying one. As you read Craig's scenario, compare it to Warren's scenario, the High D Developer pattern featured in Chapter 3, who is also a senior human resources executive. You will see that, given their style differences, they use different high-frequency behaviors to get the job done, and they have quite different motivators and demotivators. Note also that they are in very different work cultures, i.e., Craig in a college and Warren in a construction company.

Craig started his career as a middle school language arts teacher but changed to personnel work after five years. Interestingly, he left teaching because he felt there were too many administrative restrictions that kept him from doing his best. This is not a surprising sentiment coming from an Investigator style, which thrives on achievement and independent action. Over the years, Craig has worked in several human resources positions, including one as a labor negotiator. His last three jobs have been as the top human resources officer in his organization.

Craig's role is broader than that of the typical human resources executive since he is also responsible for the college's facilities and campus mail services. In the human resources realm, Craig is responsible for supervising several staff members, hiring non-academic staff, maintaining employee records, developing human resources policies and procedures, sustaining good employee relations, and providing management

© 2001 by Inscape Publishing, Inc. All rights reserved. DiSC is a registered trademark of Inscape Publishing, Inc.

development and training. He also serves as a member of the college executive committee, the group responsible for developing the college's overall operating plans and policies.

The behaviors Craig routinely uses on this job closely align with what you would expect to see in someone with his High S-D-C pattern. He most frequently

- seeks new ideas and methods for getting results
- takes the initiative to start large or long-term projects
- identifies problems, subjects, or priorities needing to be discussed
- listens analytically, questioning when necessary
- resolves conflicting differences through discussion
- chooses carefully among alternatives before acting
- seeks and evaluates information before making decisions.

Craig mentioned several motivators inherent in his work as a senior human resources executive at the college. Most of them are entirely consistent with what would be appealing to someone of his DiSC® pattern. He mentioned as most motivating to him

- the autonomy of his job because he values independence
- doing a complete redesign of the human resources systems, from beginning to end, because he enjoys being responsible for complete segments of work
- the trust given to him by the college for his knowledge, experience, and judgment because he values the respect of his peers
- working on critically important issues because he needs to believe that he is contributing to the success of the college
- an atmosphere of open discussion on issues and problems faced by the college without attributing blame because he works best in a climate of collaboration

© 2001 by Inscape Publishing, Inc. All rights reserved. DiSC is a registered trademark of Inscape Publishing, Inc.

- the college president (his boss) who trusts his judgment because he does his best work when he doesn't have to worry about someone second-guessing him.

Craig cited only a few demotivators in his job. They are somewhat related to someone of his DiSC® pattern, particularly the things related to his expertise and control. He mentioned as most demotivating

- continued distractions of skimping on budget issues because he feels they are usually penny-wise and pound-foolish decisions
- supervision of areas like the mailroom and facilities because he is bored by things that do not interest him
- interference by others in the organization in the management of his division because he feels that he knows more about the issues at hand than they but still has to accommodate them.

As you read Craig's scenario, did you find his motivators and demotivators similar to yours? If not, how are they different? Can you see yourself performing your work in a similar way?

Owen—Agent Pattern (High S, moderately High I)

Owen's most productive and satisfying job was as a loss-control consultant in a regional office of a large insurance company. He just recently retired and is still doing some independent consulting in the same field. He considered it the perfect job for someone of his Agent pattern. He started in the company as a new college graduate with a degree in economics and went on to spend his entire working career there. He had no sights on upper management or promotion to supervision, so he stayed in the same job for his entire career. (This is quite unusual in a time when most people switch jobs six to eight times in a career.) That is not to say that he did not grow or change—he did. He just liked being out in the field, seeing customers, and doing his job.

© 2001 by Inscape Publishing, Inc. All rights reserved. DiSC is a registered trademark of Inscape Publishing, Inc.

The core of Owen's job was safety—preventing injury, damages, and other losses due to unsafe practices or conditions in his customers' plants, warehouses, retail stores, and other settings. Good loss prevention benefited the customer in reduced insurance premiums, safety of personnel, and prevention of damage to materials and equipment. His employer benefited by reduced claims and by having satisfied customers.

Owen's main duties were to carefully inspect and observe customers' properties and worker practices for any conditions that could lead to worker or customer injury or loss from fire or explosion. Owen wrote reports of his inspections and briefed his customers on what they could do to prevent or fix problems. He also gave training sessions to customers' employees and safety representatives.

Owen says that the job of loss-control consultant is a real juggling act. He had to be exact and firm in observing and reporting potential loss conditions, but he also had to do it in a way that was engaging and non-combative. He achieved more through his influencing skills than he did by his safety expertise or position of authority. He says that people were more willing to fix things when the climate was calm and friendly. As a normally cheerful and helpful person, Owen developed many good friends within his client base over his career.

Owen cited several behaviors that he routinely used to be most effective in his loss-control consultant job. The behaviors align with what you would expect to see in someone with his High S-I pattern. However, he says that he was frequently out of his comfort zone because of the need to push for change and compliance. He most frequently

- sought new ideas and methods for getting results
- interacted with new people
- persuaded others to his point of view
- sought and evaluated information before making decisions

 • © 2001 by Inscape Publishing, Inc. All rights reserved. DiSC is a registered trademark of Inscape Publishing, Inc.

- worked cooperatively with others to complete tasks
- cited evidence emphasizing a specific point of view or desired results to be achieved.

Owen derived much enjoyment from his work as a loss-control consultant. All of the motivators he cited fit with the types of things you would expect to hear from someone with his High S-I pattern. The most motivational aspects of the job to Owen were

- being out of the office with customers most of the time because he tended to be active and non-corporate
- meeting new people every day because he enjoyed serving people and being with them and it was fun
- receiving good comments from his company's underwriters and his customers for doing a good job because it gave him a good feeling to know how much he was appreciated
- little or no pressure in the job because he did not respond well in high-pressure situations
- learning about various types of businesses because he enjoyed learning new things
- being free to set his own schedule because he liked being his own boss and doing what had to be done when it needed to be done.

The demotivators of Owen's loss-control consultant job are very consistent with what you would expect from someone with his High S-I Agent behavior pattern. They were

- internal people in the company who made little effort to understand his situation and his customers' needs because their lack of cooperation negatively affected his hard work and professionalism
- lack of cooperation or follow-through by some customers because even though he tried to be helpful they didn't seem to care

© 2001 by Inscape Publishing, Inc. All rights reserved. DiSC is a registered trademark of Inscape Publishing, Inc.

- for reasons out of his control, losing long-term customers with whom he had personal, friendly relationships.

As you read Owen's scenario, did you find his motivators and demotivators similar to yours? If not, how are they different? Can you see yourself performing your work in a similar way?

Jill—Achiever Pattern (High S, High D)

Jill is a High S-D Achiever pattern, another one of the more rare behavioral blends. She combines the stability orientation of the High S with the achievement orientation of a High D. The pattern comprises only about 1 percent of the general population. Jill stated that her most productive and satisfying job is her current one as project manager in a training publications company. The company sells packaged and online training programs to corporate and governmental users.

Jill's main duty involves guiding the development and publication of training programs through a rather complex and sometimes painful process, starting with an idea and ending with a training program that works in a corporate classroom. Jill earned a promotion to this job about two years ago. Before that, she was a production assistant, her first job after college where she earned a degree in English literature. At first, Jill did not see a tight connection between her degree and her job, but now she does because she applies her English skills in a number of ways, including input on video character development, scripting, and editing.

Jill's specific job duties vary greatly. She develops project plans with the product managers, coordinates and leads creative meetings with course designers and subject matter experts, coordinates product reviews and edits, coordinates product beta tests, and manages the product packaging and production. She is very committed to doing an excellent job and being accountable for her work.

88 • © 2001 by Inscape Publishing, Inc. All rights reserved. DiSC is a registered trademark of Inscape Publishing, Inc.

Jill is the happiest when her projects wind up on the warehouse shelf, ready for sale. Getting them there is the big challenge because there are so many variables that can go wrong, e.g., personalities, resource shortages, and conflicts. Sometimes she is tempted to push people aside and do the work herself, but that would be disastrous because she would never be able to do the work and manage the projects as well.

In her job, Jill routinely uses a variety of behaviors that are typical of someone with her High S-D Achiever behavior pattern. The job is a blend of people and production, and the extent that she does both well leads to a high level of productivity. Behaviors she uses most frequently include

- taking the initiative to start large or long-term projects
- working cooperatively with others to get the job done
- monitoring and maintaining key requirements for producing a quality product
- identifying problems, subjects, or priorities needing to be discussed and acted upon
- remaining neutral (at least initially) when conflicts arise
- displaying restraint when feeling anxious or impatient
- making unpopular decisions needed to complete a task or activity.

Jill loves her job because there are many motivators inherent in the work. Every day is a challenge and very rewarding. She said that her biggest motivators are

- setting her own goals and taking accountability for her work because she enjoys producing results
- being able to perform high-quality work because that is the way she does things all the time
- seeing things go from an idea to an actual product because the process is complex, creative, and stimulating

© 2001 by Inscape Publishing, Inc. All rights reserved. DiSC is a registered trademark of Inscape Publishing, Inc.

- working with bright, creative people because the conversations, the humor, and just being around them is so stimulating
- being recognized and rewarded by her manager for doing excellent work because she is driven by accomplishment.

On the demotivating side, Jill reported several things that make work unpleasant at times. Her biggest demotivators are

- other people trying to control her projects or change her project plans because she wants to be fully in charge and accountable for the desired results
- people who do not perform or follow through on their commitments because non-performance slows things down and results in poor quality
- pressure to compromise on her approach to doing things because it kind of feels like she is giving up on what she believes in.

As you read Jill's scenario, did you find her motivators and demotivators similar to yours? If not, how are they different? Can you see yourself performing your work in a similar way?

Finding the Fit: Suitable Jobs for a High S

What are the career fields, jobs, or work environments that are most suitable for the High Steadiness tendency? As we know, High Ss thrive in situations where they can achieve stability and accomplish tasks by cooperating with others. They are supportive, respectful, willing, dependable, and agreeable. Because of this, High Ss should consider jobs and workplaces where they can

- work in a steady, predictable, and orderly manner
- form personal, long-term relationships with their employers and coworkers

- work harmoniously and cooperatively with others to achieve common results
- minimize any kind of risk, especially any kind of personal exposure or being in the limelight
- perform work in conventional and proven ways
- make decisions through group consensus, rather than strictly on their own
- hold their opinions to themselves or to their close friends and family members
- show loyalty to the organizations, their leaders, and others
- show patience and empathy for people and situations
- respect tradition.

High Ss would most likely be least comfortable in work cultures and jobs where

- they are not appreciated for their efforts
- the work involves higher levels of risk, both emotional and physical
- conflict abounds
- unsteadiness or uncertainty prevails
- the general tone is disruptive and noisy
- behavior is nonconforming and erratic
- people are overly direct, aggressive, or dominant.

As we have discussed, we can be successful in any job, regardless of our behavioral style, so long as we adapt to the role requirements of our job. However, we also know that it makes good sense to get into a job that is a good fit at the outset because some jobs or roles may require more versatility from you than you are prepared to give. That said, following are some examples of careers and jobs most likely to be attractive to a High S:

- elementary school teacher
- secondary school teacher

- game, fish, or forestry worker
- customer service representative
- social worker
- clergyperson
- financial service worker
- restaurant server or host
- medical doctor (family practitioner, pediatrician)
- nurse/medical assistant/nursing assistant
- dentist/dental assistant
- occupational therapist
- residential and community service agent
- personal/administrative assistant
- receptionist
- records administrator or manager
- insurance agent
- librarian
- human resources representative, especially employee relations
- recreation leader
- homemaker
- child-care attendant
- kindergarten/preschool teacher
- veterinarian
- family lawyer
- engineer
- parole officer/corrections officer
- truck or delivery driver
- government agency worker
- retail cashier/bank teller.

The Link Between Your Pattern and Job or Culture Requirements

It is important to select a career or job and work culture that is a good match for your style. If they do not fit, you may be in for tough times. For example, if you were a High S-I pattern and interested in being a librarian, you would probably be most happy working in a school or community library where you could meet and serve people of all ages who have many different needs. However, if you wound up in the resources library of a large corporation, there is a chance that your needs would not be met because of the formal, impersonal, task-oriented nature of such a place.

Another example of a non-fit is the case of Pamela, the High S Specialist pattern featured in this chapter. Stylewise, she was perfectly suited for the job of medical assistant, and she enjoyed many years working in a medical office culture that was comfortable for her. The doctor and her coworkers there were all very amiable and patient-oriented. What if Pamela changed jobs and worked in an impersonal work culture led by a dominant, direct, and fast-paced High D doctor? Chances are she would be unhappy and may not last long there.

Chapter Summary

People with the High S behavioral style are typically supportive, respectful, willing, dependable, and agreeable. They prefer jobs and work environments where they can work in a steady, predictable, and orderly manner, form lasting relationships with their employer and coworkers, and work harmoniously and cooperatively with others. As with people of the other DiSC® classical patterns, people of the various High S DiSC® patterns, i.e., Agent, Specialist, Achiever, and Perfectionist, should give thoughtful consideration to the specific job and

© 2001 by Inscape Publishing, Inc. All rights reserved. DiSC is a registered trademark of Inscape Publishing, Inc.

work culture they choose. This is because of the blended nature of the various patterns. For example, a person with a High S-I Agent pattern would do well in a direct service job, but would probably feel considerable stress stretching and redirecting to the roles of an accountant. Ultimately, when we are able to be in a job that fits well, we usually feel happy and are more effective.

Some Things to Think About

As you read the scenarios of the High S people in this chapter, did you see a high degree of similarity between you and them? If so, what did you see that seemed true for you? If not, what was different for you?

_____

_____

_____

_____

What jobs, past or present, have you had where you experienced similar style-related motivators? How did they affect your job satisfaction and effectiveness?

_____

_____

_____

_____

What jobs, past or present, have you had where there were far more style-related demotivators than there were motivators? How did this affect your job satisfaction and effectiveness?

_____

_____

_____

_____

If you are a High S and searching for a good fit job or career field, what kinds of work do you think would be a good fit for you, assuming you were otherwise fully qualified? If not fully qualified, what would it take for you to be so?

_____

_____

_____

_____

If you are a High S and in a job that is not a good fit, how can you adapt (see Chapter 7) or change things to make it a better fit?

_____

_____

_____

_____

The High C:
"Before we take action on this, I want to assess the pros and cons to be sure we make the right decision!"

Introduction

In this chapter, you will get a view of those who have the High C, Conscientiousness, tendency or style. High Cs thrive in situations where they can work within circumstances to ensure quality and accuracy. We will cover their main motivators and demotivators, and how they typically affect others in the work environment. We will then cover the specific jobs and work cultures that would be a good fit for High Cs, and we will cover the kinds of situations and jobs that would be demotivating for them.

Review of the Conscientiousness Style

The Conscientiousness tendency, or High C style, is another of the four main behavioral domains Dr. William Marston identified in his research. Marston originally named the C tendency compliant, but contemporary users saw the word as a negative description and changed it. After all, who would claim to be compliant? Actually, what Marston meant was that High Cs are compliant to their own internal standards. Some DISC publishers use the term *cautious*. I prefer the term *conscientiousness*, a more positively descriptive term used by Inscape Publishing in its assessments and materials.

When you observe the typical High C, you will see behavior characterized by attention to standards and details, analytical thinking, accuracy, diplomacy, and indirect approaches to conflict. They have a preference to detach from others and adapt to people and circumstances around them. Those with a high level of conscientiousness behavior show many interrelated strengths. In general, they tend to

- pay attention to key directives and maintain standards
- be detail-oriented and exacting in their approach
- carefully and unemotionally weigh the pros and cons of an issue before deciding
- perform work thoroughly and accurately
- be dependable and follow through on commitments
- focus on outcomes and expectations.

As with the other style tendencies, High Cs can show a range of limiting behaviors that can hinder their effectiveness. If not self-managed well, High Cs tend to

- be overly critical of themselves and others
- be indecisive due to the need for more analysis, i.e., analysis paralysis

- be too reliant on structured problem solving and closed to gut solutions
- be unwilling to change their approach to accommodate others
- overuse conservative thinking, modesty, and standard procedures
- be complex and overly serious.

There are actually four different High C behavior patterns, or blends, in the Conscientiousness family. As you read the brief descriptions of each, note the shape of the graph and the intensity (the higher the plot point, the more noticeable that behavior) of each of the behavioral tendencies.

People with the **Objective Thinker pattern** strive to apply their highly developed critical thinking abilities. They emphasize the importance of facts when drawing conclusions and planning actions and seek corrections and accuracy in all that they do. They thrive in situations where they can define, clarify, obtain, evaluate, and test information. They are particularly uncomfortable with aggressive people and conflict.

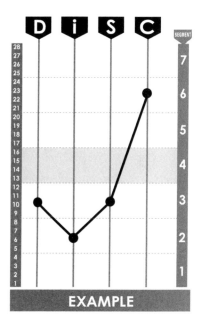

Objective Thinker

© 2001 by Inscape Publishing, Inc. All rights reserved. DiSC is a registered trademark of Inscape Publishing, Inc.

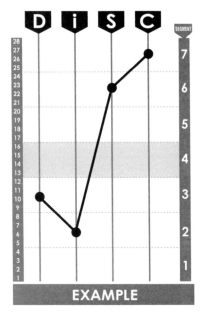

Perfectionist

Those with the **Perfectionist pattern** are systematic, precise thinkers and follow procedure in both their personal and work lives. They are extremely conscientious and work well in situations that involve details and accuracy. Perfectionists are most comfortable in a clearly defined work environment where they know the quality expectations, time requirements, and evaluation procedures of their work.

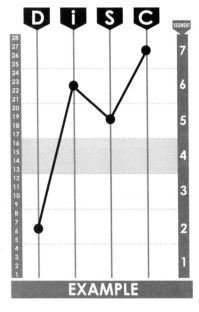

Practitioner

People with the **Practitioner pattern** typically value being proficient in specialized areas. Because Practitioners have three behavioral tendencies at play, there are fewer of them in the general population. They often give the impression to others that they know something about everything. This is particularly evident when, because of their higher I, they tend to verbalize their knowledge on a variety of subjects. Practitioners do best in jobs where they can display their proficiency and specialization and solve both technical and people problems.

 © 2001 by Inscape Publishing, Inc. All rights reserved. DiSC is a registered trademark of Inscape Publishing, Inc.

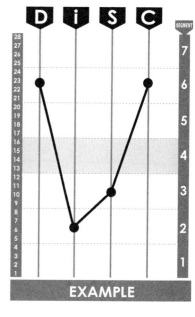

EXAMPLE

Creative

People with the **Creative pattern** (This pattern appears in Chapter 3 as well) do best in environments where they can be dominant and contribute unique accomplishments. They prefer situations where they can design or initiate change. They do best in jobs where they have the freedom to explore and have the authority to examine and test their findings through action.

High C Behavioral Pattern People at Work: Some Real-Life Scenarios

As you will recall from previous chapters, I did research with people about what motivated or demotivated them in a job where they were both satisfied and effective. I wrote the scenarios to help you gain a view of what it is like for people of certain styles to work in various jobs. This information could be enormously valuable to you as you consider your own job needs. When you read the following High C scenarios, put yourself into the stories and ask yourself the following:

- If I were in this job, would I approach it in the same way? Why? Why not?
- Would the same things motivate me? Why? Why not?
- Would the same things demotivate me? Why? Why not?
- Do I know anyone like this? If so, who? What kind of work do they do?

© 2001 by Inscape Publishing, Inc. All rights reserved. DiSC is a registered trademark of Inscape Publishing, Inc. •

By answering the questions, you will begin to understand your own behaviors and motives better and make important connections about the kind of work you do now, or might enjoy doing, and how you do or would approach your work.

Ray—Objective Thinker Pattern (Pure High C)

Ray has a High C behavior pattern. He says that his most productive and satisfying job is that of a training manager in a medium-sized (about 800 employees) governmental agency. Ray's organization provides a direct service to the public and enjoys an excellent reputation for the quality of its service.

Ray is the manager of a three-person training group within the human resources department. His duties vary widely. They include supervisory leadership of his people, budget management, strategic planning for the organization, customer service training, supervisory training, leadership development, program design and development, and coordinating outside suppliers and resources.

For most of his career, Ray has been either a teacher in public schools or a trainer in business and government. He enjoys classroom teaching, but finds it difficult because he must stretch from his shy, low-key, formal High C style to be more outgoing and verbally expressive. A successful day in the classroom can be quite exhausting for Ray. He is, however, quite willing and able to be flexible. It just takes a lot out of him.

Therefore, it should come as no surprise that Ray's favorite type of work, and his strong suit, is conceptualizing and planning. He is very detail-oriented and accurate in everything he does. For this reason, Ray facilitates the organization's strategic planning process and develops and publishes its updated five-year plan annually. The work is complex and

 • © 2001 by Inscape Publishing, Inc. All rights reserved. DiSC is a registered trademark of Inscape Publishing, Inc.

detailed, both of which appeal to Ray. This work takes him away from the traditional role of trainer, but he is quite willing to hire others to do the classroom work. This illustrates the distinct value that people can contribute to their organizations *vis-à-vis* their behavioral styles.

In addition to his High C, Ray also has a mid-level D that serves him well in a number of roles that he must perform. As the group's leader, he must initiate and complete important projects and activities. In addition, it helps to have a bit of a higher D in his strategic planning role because the high-powered senior executives in the planning process are not shy about expressing their views and wanting to prevail. Ray needs a bit of a backbone to direct and control these people to achieve positive outcomes that reflect the total group's thinking.

When Ray discussed the behaviors he uses most often in his training job, he cited behaviors that are very much in tune with the behavioral realm of the High C. He most frequently

- seeks and evaluates information before making decisions
- identifies problems, subjects, or priorities for discussion
- supplies information without showing an opinion
- cites evidence emphasizing a specific point of view or desired results
- stays at the same physical location most of the time
- listens analytically, questioning when necessary
- chooses carefully among alternatives before acting.

When discussing his favorite job as a training manager, Ray cited many motivators that are inherent in his work. They are very consistent with those of Ray's High C pattern. The most motivational aspects of the job are

- seeing things work because he gets a great sense of satisfaction to see his plans implemented and working

© 2001 by Inscape Publishing, Inc. All rights reserved. DiSC is a registered trademark of Inscape Publishing, Inc.

- seeing people learn and grow in their competency because it makes him feel that what he does has meaning
- taking an idea from conception to completion because he likes to see tangible results—something he can point to and say, "I did that"
- learning how to apply new computer tools/software and other resources because it keeps him fresh, interested, and growing.

Ray mentioned only two demotivators that are a part of his training manager job. Both would be inherently demotivating to someone with his High C Conscientiousness behavior pattern. Most demotivating are

- senior management not taking his work seriously because he believes in what he is doing, but they sometimes do not
- a lack of follow-through on some of the plans he develops because there is a lot more said than done.

As you read Ray's scenario, did you find his motivators and demotivators similar to yours? If not, how are they different? Can you see yourself performing your work in a similar way?

Julie—Perfectionist Pattern (High C, High S)

Julie says her present job of bank teller in a small branch office of a regional banking chain is her most productive and satisfying one. She has had two other major jobs in her working career. Her first was that of an elementary school teacher for five years. Then, when she began her family, she was a full-time homemaker. After several years in this role, she started working as a bank teller. While a bank teller, Julie has occasionally thought about going back to teaching, especially because she could double her salary. However, the banking job calls her, mainly because it is relatively pressure-free, she enjoys the work so much, and she loves serving her customers.

 © 2001 by Inscape Publishing, Inc. All rights reserved. DiSC is a registered trademark of Inscape Publishing, Inc.

Julie's duties are typical for those of a bank teller. She works the service counter most of the time helping customers with bank deposits, check cashing, money orders, cashier's checks, wire transfers, currency exchanges, and other banking services. When she senses that a customer has a need for a specific service, like a car loan, she makes such a recommendation and refers the customer to a banking officer. Julie says the four most important skills of a bank teller are good people skills, a strong detail orientation, good clerical abilities, and the ability to operate computers and other banking machines.

On the surface, the teller job might appear to be fairly routine and predictable. Even so, Julie says she always has to be alert for things that don't fit the pattern, like fraudulent checks, closed accounts, and expired bankcards. When this occurs, the teller must crank up assertiveness and settle the problem without upsetting the customer too much. In addition, the beginning cash and the withdrawals and deposits of her cash drawer must balance to the penny every day!

Julie mentioned several behaviors that serve her well in her day-to-day work as a bank teller. They are quite consistent with a person of her High C-S behavior pattern. Most frequently she
- shows understanding of others by responding to their feelings
- works cooperatively with others to complete tasks
- cooperates with others to solve problems
- enjoys interacting with people who have different styles
- responds optimistically to people's concerns and problems
- performs repetitive tasks without losing motivation
- stays at the same physical location most of the time.

When discussing her favorite job, Julie mentioned several motivators inherent in her bank teller job. These motivators are very consistent with the needs of someone with High C-S Perfectionist behavior pattern. The most motivational aspects of the job are

© 2001 by Inscape Publishing, Inc. All rights reserved. DiSC is a registered trademark of Inscape Publishing, Inc.

- interacting with many customers all day long because she gets to know them well and can tease them, care about them, and feel a part of their lives
- being able to help customers solve problems with their checkbook because it gives her a good feeling when she can help someone
- getting to know so many kinds of people because it makes her job interesting and fun
- being able to balance to the penny each day because balancing makes her feel that she is doing things right.

Strangely, when compared to others featured in this book, Julie mentioned only one job demotivator: The requirement to cross-sell bank products to her customers because she is not comfortable selling. She said, "Actually, I don't really sell…. I just listen to the customer, and if there is a product we have that would help them, I tell them about it." (*Author's note: Julie may not know it, but she has just defined the essence of good selling—recommending products or services that fill a customer's need!*)

As you read Julie's scenario did you find her motivators and demotivators to be similar to yours? If not, how are they different? Can you see yourself performing your work in a similar way?

Kent—Practitioner Pattern (High C, High I, moderately High S)

Kent says that his current job as a construction project manager is his favorite. He enjoys the work and, according to the feedback he has received from others, performs it well. Kent's employer is a medium-sized general contractor who specializes in building small retail strip-malls and stand-alone commercial buildings.

Kent has worked for this company for seven years. He joined them right after graduating from college with a degree in construction

• © 2001 by Inscape Publishing, Inc. All rights reserved. DiSC is a registered trademark of Inscape Publishing, Inc.

management. His first job there was as an estimator, where he worked with detailed construction plans to estimate the time and materials needed to complete various projects. After two years, he was promoted to assistant project manager where his main job was to support the project managers in their duties and perform the administrative tasks associated with projects, e.g., change orders and submittals.

Kent made project manager after five years in the company. He loves his job because of the people he works with and the constant challenge of constructing good quality buildings on time and on budget. Kent is ultimately responsible for the profitability of each project he manages. Since there are many things that can go wrong—work quality issues, cost overruns on labor and materials, accidents—the job brings a fair amount of pressure. Kent says you have to "plan your work, and work your plan," if you are going to be a successful project manager.

Kent performs a range of duties as a project manager. His main ones include supporting the sales development, bidding process for the project, managing owner/architect relationships, administering contracts, managing the project budget, scheduling projects, overseeing job safety and project quality, and leading the project team (estimators, assistant project managers, and superintendents) in the performance of their duties.

From beginning to end, a construction project has a certain flow to it. The key to successful project management is good planning, effective communication, and good relationships with people—all things Kent considers his personal strengths. The behaviors Kent uses most frequently in his job are quite consistent with someone of his High C-I-S Practitioner behavior pattern:

- monitors and maintains key requirements for quality and safety

© 2001 by Inscape Publishing, Inc. All rights reserved. DiSC is a registered trademark of Inscape Publishing, Inc.

- identifies problems, subjects, or priorities needing to be discussed and resolved
- listens analytically, questioning when necessary
- makes unpopular decisions needed to complete a task or activity
- cooperates with others when solving problems
- exercises caution and calculates risks before acting
- resolves conflicting differences through discussion.

As noted, Kent loves his project manager job because of its many motivating aspects. Most of them are the kinds of things that would appeal to someone of his behavior pattern. He mentioned as motivators the following:

- taking a project from the initial plan to a quality building because he enjoys the process and he is good at it
- working with his colleagues on the project team because they get along well and they are mostly all peak performers and contribute great value to the project
- having promotion opportunities in his company because it is important for him to be recognized and rewarded for his expertise and competence
- accessing the wide variety of tasks and responsibilities because they challenge his expertise and problem-solving abilities
- constantly having to learn new techniques and concepts because he loves to learn and challenge himself to even better performance.

As with most people, Kent has experienced some demotivators on his job:

- poor performance on the part of some people and sub-contractors because it indicates a lack of professionalism and self-discipline

 © 2001 by Inscape Publishing, Inc. All rights reserved. DiSC is a registered trademark of Inscape Publishing, Inc.

- problems and issues come up that he should have prevented because he doesn't like to admit incompetence when things go wrong
- sudden changes required in the project due to unforeseen events like material delays because it upsets project plans and organization.

As you read Kent's scenario, did you find his motivators and demotivators to be similar to yours? If not, how are they different? Can you see yourself performing your work in a similar way?

Eileen—Creative Pattern (High C, High D)

Although we have written in Chapter 3 about Larry, another Creative pattern, Eileen's case shows a reverse set of Creative pattern behaviors. She has a stronger orientation to her High C side than her High D side. I thought it would be interesting to present her case as well, since she has a very different approach to things.

Eileen is a contract specialist in a large, global company. In a broad sense, her job is similar to that of a purchasing agent. She chose the contract specialist job as her most satisfying and productive one because it is such a good fit with her temperament and interests. She has had this job for about seven years. For a number of years prior to that, she was an administrative coordinator in the law department of the same firm.

Eileen's job is complex and pressure-filled. She manages contractual relationships with over 350 varied suppliers who provide some sort of materials or services to her company. Because of many details and issues that come up, Eileen says she is "always behind." She deals with many individuals—both internal customers and outside suppliers—each day, oftentimes in stressful circumstances. Attending to their needs and issues requires a high level of detail orientation, emotional control,

© 2001 by Inscape Publishing, Inc. All rights reserved. DiSC is a registered trademark of Inscape Publishing, Inc.

and sensitivity. She states that while her company wants to deal with suppliers as partners, she must also be alert for the times when supplier behavior could be harmful to her firm.

The job is complex because it involves a number of duties that require a command of details, financial calculations, and relationships. Specifically, Eileen negotiates prices, arranges for usage and reproduction licenses, manages supply and distribution arrangements, issues/reissues supplier contracts, processes invoice payment approvals, evaluates suppliers, and manages the overall buying and contracting process. Eileen says she has done her job well when she

- negotiates the best financial value for the company
- reduces risk from license and copyright violations
- satisfies her internal customers by getting them what they want
- builds strong and lasting relationships with preferred suppliers.

Eileen described several behaviors she consistently uses in the day-to-day performance of her job. They align well with someone of her High C-D behavior pattern, particularly in the kind of work she does. She most frequently

- seeks and evaluates information before making decisions
- identifies problems, subjects, or priorities that need to be discussed
- listens analytically, questioning when necessary
- exercises caution and calculates risks before acting
- chooses carefully among alternatives before acting
- facilitates interaction between people to achieve results.

Eileen loves being a contract specialist and mentioned several aspects of her work that are most motivating to her:

 © 2001 by Inscape Publishing, Inc. All rights reserved. DiSC is a registered trademark of Inscape Publishing, Inc.

- assisting with or promoting solutions to her internal customers because she likes the challenges inherent in problem-solving work
- handling detail-oriented, legalistic work because she likes to accomplish difficult tasks
- meeting people from around the world because they are interesting and represent different experiences than hers
- creating win-win agreements for both parties because it creates a means for both parties to grow and expand on their business relationship
- making a difference because she gets enjoyment from producing something valuable to her company and its people.

Eileen mentioned only two major demotivators of her job as a contract specialist:

- suppliers who have little or no business ethics because she expects the same high standard of behavior from others that she expects from herself
- lazy people who cannot or will not do their jobs well and who negatively affect others and her because, again, she expects the same from others that she expects from herself.

As you read Eileen's scenario, did you find her motivators and demotivators to be similar to yours? If not, how are they different? Can you see yourself performing your work in a similar way?

Finding the Fit: Suitable Jobs for a High C

So, what are the career fields or jobs that are most suitable for the High C? As we know, people who are high in this behavior dimension thrive in situations where they can work within circumstances to ensure quality and accuracy. High Cs possess many important behavioral strengths. They are industrious, persistent, serious, exacting, and orderly. Because of these, they would do well to consider career fields, jobs, and workplaces where they can

- apply their own structures, methods, and models within the expectations of the work
- work in a relatively calm, organized workplace with a minimum of socializing
- perform work at high standards of quality and precision and consistently meet those standards over time
- be appreciated for their correctness and contributions to the reliability and quality of outcomes
- be free of unwarranted personal criticism from others
- be relatively free of changes and surprises where they will not have to wing it
- focus on processes, i.e., how things work.

High Cs would most likely be least comfortable in work cultures and jobs where

- mistakes are tolerated
- illogical decisions are made
- people are careless about time and punctuality
- inadequate research is done before moving ahead on things
- pressure to move quickly and sudden deadlines prevail
- people are excessively loud, boisterous, and extroverted.

As we have discussed, you can be successful in any job, regardless of your behavioral style, so long as you adapt to the role requirements of your job. However, we also know that it makes good sense to get into a job that is a good fit at the outset because some jobs and roles may require more versatility from you than you are prepared to give. That said, the following are some examples of careers and jobs most likely to be attractive for High Cs:

- administrator (any industry)
- forecaster (political pollsters, weather, etc.)
- engineer (all types)
- dentist
- nurse
- psychotherapist/psychologist
- forestry/environmental worker
- information technology worker
- business/organizational systems analyst
- computer programmer
- software designer
- analyst (data, intelligence, etc.)
- actuary
- researcher
- librarian
- clergyperson
- attorney
- inventor
- financial manager
- banker
- accountant/auditor
- bookkeeper
- artist/sculptor
- architect
- construction estimator/scheduler/project manager
- carpenter
- civil servant
- musician
- writer
- journalist
- truck driver

- police officer
- military officer or enlisted person in technical fields
- special agent (e.g., Federal Bureau of Investigation; Bureau of Alcohol, Tobacco, Firearms, and Explosives).

The Link Between Your Pattern and Job or Culture Requirements

Simply having a good fit between your job and your style could be a problem if you work in a culture that doesn't fit. For example, as a calm, perfectionistic, deliberate High C, you would feel completely out of place in an organizational culture that values action over thought, and where high-energy, in-your-face communication rules the day. This is critical for you to consider because just as you have your needs and preferences, organizations have theirs.

If you were a low-key, serious, analytical High C Objective Thinker pattern and were placed behind the scenes doing computer programming in an organization's information technology department, chances are you would be very happy and productive. You would likely be associated with other High Cs, focused on highly detailed, deliberate, process-oriented computer and software outputs—a great match!

However, what if you had to work at the company's help desk where customers from throughout the company call in for support with computer problems? They would want friendly, responsive service and instant solutions. Would you enjoy the work as much? Probably not. Chances are that kind of work would require you to constantly stretch and redirect your behaviors way out of your comfort zone to meet the requirements of this problem-solver role. Over time, this job would likely take its toll in your energy and drive to excel.

 © 2001 by Inscape Publishing, Inc. All rights reserved. DiSC is a registered trademark of Inscape Publishing, Inc.

What if you were a High C-I Appraiser pattern? The help-desk function would likely be a good job for you. You could apply your analytical talents, and you would have a chance to talk with people, solve their problems, and enjoy their positive feedback when you get them up and running. Another great match!

Chapter Summary

Those with the High C behavioral style typically pay attention to detail, are detail-oriented and exacting in their work, carefully weigh the pros and cons when making a decision, and perform their work thoroughly and accurately. They thrive in jobs and environments where they can apply their own structure, standards, and methods within work expectations; work in a relatively calm, organized workplace with a minimum of socializing; and perform work at high standards of quality and precision and consistently meet those standards over time. Depending on one's specific DiSC® classical pattern, i.e., Creative, Objective Thinker, Appraiser, or Perfectionist, an individual should choose a job or career that fits best. For example, a person with a pure High C Objective Thinker pattern would probably have difficulty stretching and redirecting to the roles of a street cop, whereas a High C-D Creative pattern would feel very much at home with the investigative analysis and assertiveness required in that job. Clearly, when there is a fit we have a much better chance of being happier and more productive in our work.

© 2001 by Inscape Publishing, Inc. All rights reserved. DiSC is a registered trademark of Inscape Publishing, Inc.

Some Things to Think About

As you read the scenarios of the High C people in this chapter, did you see a high degree of similarity between you and them? If so, what did you see that seemed true for you? If not, what was different for you?

_____

_____

_____

_____

What jobs, past or present, have you had where you experienced similar style-related motivators? How did they affect your job satisfaction and effectiveness?

_____

_____

_____

_____

What jobs, past or present, have you had where there were far more style-related demotivators than there were motivators? How did this affect your job satisfaction and effectiveness?

_____

_____

_____

_____

If you are a High C and searching for a good fit job or career field, what kinds of work do you think would be a good fit for you, assuming you were otherwise fully qualified? If not fully qualified, what would it take for you to be so?

_____

_____

_____

_____

If you are a High C and in a job that is not a good fit, how can you adapt (see Chapter 7) or change things to make it a better fit?

_____

_____

_____

_____

Practicing Adaptability:

"To be or not to be?
That is the question...
and the opportunity."

Introduction

In this chapter, you will learn about how to adapt your behavior temporarily to deal skillfully with various people and situations. We will cover the purpose, power, and benefits of adaptability. Then, we will discuss the particular challenges that people of the various DiSC® patterns have in being adaptive. Lastly, you will learn two important skills: how to identify the DISC behavioral style of others and how to create workable adaptability strategies to deal with them effectively.

What Is Adaptability, and Why Is It So Important?

Each of us is unique. We all have different personalities, drives, needs, and expectations. The successful person is self-aware and able, through self-monitoring and self-management, to manage these characteristics in ways that help build a happy and productive life. This self-awareness is the radar that allows us to navigate through life, dealing effectively with people and situations. We are mindful about conditions around us and make an effort to deal with them as best we can.

So what is this capability? It is adaptability, the will and the skill to deal effectively with the requirements of a situation or relationship in ways that are not typical of your behavioral style. However, being adaptive is not as easy as it sounds because our tendency is to want to do what is most natural and comfortable for us, to do what we feel like doing, and to do what meets our needs. The adaptive person, however, does what is the best thing for the moment and what meets the needs of the situation, even if there is a little pain leaving one's comfort zone.

People who consistently adjust their personal styles to meet the requirements of various work situations, and the needs of others, are a prized resource in any organization or setting. They tend to perform their jobs better, serve their customers better, and create better working relationships.

General Adaptability

There are two types of adaptability. First, there is the general form of adaptability when people, no matter what their behavioral styles, make an effort to create good interpersonal relationships with others and make things work. They seem to be naturally flexible. You have probably seen them at work, in school, and in your personal life. I know that I have. Not that I can claim any special gift of adaptability, but I do remember noting these kinds of people in my past and saying to myself, "I want to be like them."

At this level of adaptability, regardless of their personal DISC behavioral style, you will see people with a high level of self-awareness and self-regulation of their behaviors. They routinely deal well with situations and people. They are focused on the other person's needs, as much as their own, and they want to make the relationships work.

Two prominent psychologists, Daniel Goleman, author of *Emotional Intelligence*, and Dr. Paul Pearsall, author of *The Last Self-Help Book You'll Ever Need*, comment about this important skill in their writings. They say the same thing in different ways. Goleman maintains that, for relationships to work, people have to invest in each other, i.e., give up something of themselves to make things work. Said another way, Pearsall asserts that for relationships to work, particularly in a marriage, one must be love-worthy, i.e., act in the other person's best interests, thereby earning the love or respect one wants or needs.

So, what does it look like if we were to see someone exercising this special talent? Listed below are several general adaptability behaviors that are typical of these flexible people. As you read them, think about the times when you were, or were not, adaptive. What helped or hindered your efforts to be so? Typically, people who are adaptive

- try to establish win-win relationships
- are open to others' ideas and are flexible in dealing with issues
- give the impression to others that they want to get along, no matter what the other person's style
- influence others through the force of their personality, rather than through their position power ("I'm the boss!") or their technical power ("I have unique knowledge that you don't!")

- make sure that others around them are at ease
- easily handle situations where they feel uncomfortable
- pay attention to what others say or do
- show patience and practice good listening with others
- are concerned about other people's well-being.

Recap of DISC Behavioral Tendencies

In this chapter, you will be reading a lot about people of the four DISC tendencies and how they adapt in the real world. Just as a refresher, so that you don't have to keep paging back, I've listed, from Chapter 2, the main points of each behavioral style below:

- **Dominant (D)** style people are determined, straightforward, and motivated by competitive opportunities and by producing results. People who display this approach tend to overcome unfavorable obstacles that block their way. They like a challenge. They tend to be assertive, independent, decisive, and direct. They get demotivated when others try to control them or take advantage of them in any way. They tend to thrive in jobs and environments where they are in charge and can take responsibility for producing results.

- Another unique expression of behavior is the **Influence (I)** tendency. People of this style tend to focus their energies on influencing or persuading others in favorable situations. They tend to be optimistic, emotional, talkative, and eager to please, and they seek social recognition. They become demotivated when they lose the recognition and approval of others. They tend to thrive in jobs and environments where they can interact with others and influence them through persuasion.

- People of the **Steadiness (S)** style tend to go along with others. They are low-keyed, easygoing, and typically follow through on matters because of their high need for stability. They tend to be good listeners and strive to maintain calm and peaceful relationships with others. Conflict and sudden change can be very demotivating to them because that tends to threaten their stability. People of this style tend to thrive in jobs and environments where they can serve others and contribute their specialized skills for the good of the organization.

- The fourth tendency is **Conscientiousness (C)**. People with a natural C like things done the "right" or "correct" way, as they see it. They show a high level of caution that fulfills their personal concern for accuracy. They tend to be very dependable and follow through on their agreements. They tend to act in ways that meet their own high standards of appropriate behavior and strive to reduce antagonistic factors that they would tend to see in an unfavorable environment. Personal criticism and sloppy work by others are big demotivators for the High C. They tend to thrive in jobs and environments where they can be accurate and show their expertise.

Behavioral Style-Related Adaptability Behaviors

What happens when we narrow the question of adaptability to the realm of specific behavioral styles? For starters, we know that people of each style tendency naturally possess abundant strengths; strengths serve us well in our day-to-day interactions with others. For example, High Ds are forceful and direct; High Is are sociable and persuasive; High Ss are predictable and serene; and High Cs are accurate and conventional. So, given their natural tendencies, what does it look like when people of the different behavioral styles are being adaptive? Here are some examples:

- A High D *listens carefully* without interrupting rather than impatiently urging someone to get to the point.
- A High I *shares the stage* in a social gathering rather than dominating the conversation with endless stories.
- A High S offers a *strong opinion* during a meeting rather than keeping quiet to assure peace and stability among coworkers.
- A High C makes a *timely decision* rather than endlessly sifting through more data and information to make the "right" decision.
- A High D *lets others take the lead* instead of controlling the actions and outcomes of a team initiative.
- A High I *thinks through a decision carefully* rather than making an impulsive decision that may bring unintended results.
- A High S *deals with change effectively* when change is necessary rather than hanging on to the old way of doing things.
- A High C *responds to others' needs empathically* rather than from a cool, impersonal, rational approach.

As you read these examples of people's natural behaviors, rather than their adaptive behaviors, you may have said, "Well, what's wrong with this or that behavior? I do it all the time!" Behavior, in and of itself, is not the issue. The issue is that each of us has a style, and each style has its strengths. In certain circumstances, like those above, what we would claim as one of our natural strengths, carried to an extreme, could be a limitation. Therefore, to be effective, we need to be aware of situations, sense what behaviors are most fitting at the time, and apply them, adapting as well as we can to those circumstances.

Let me give you an example. Some years ago, I worked as a product manager in a global training company (the place where we "hugged in the hallways"). My job was interesting and quite broad in its scope, ranging from product design and development to sales and marketing support. As such, I came into daily contact with a number of people throughout the company who performed various functions like writing, word processing, packaging, inventory control, warehousing, customer service, and sales.

During my four years at the company, we had two major layoffs where several people—about 10 percent of the workforce—were let go due to slow sales and other business conditions. Fortunately, I never made either of the termination lists. Each time, however, I wondered about those who did. I asked myself, "Why them, why not me?"

As I looked a bit deeper into things, I realized that, while a few lost their jobs because their skills and contributions were no longer needed, most were let go for a different reason. They had a reputation in the company for being hard to get along with. Quite simply, no matter what their personal behavioral style, they were not flexible. They consistently wanted to do things their way. Their emotional drives, i.e., their goals and fears, were so strong that in their self-protection and survival efforts, they became ineffective performers. When working with them you never really knew what to expect—cooperation or no help. As a result, they were expendable. The company used these situations to thin the herd, believing that if you are not part of the solution you are part of the problem. Very simply, people who could not adjust did not make it.

In looking at your own career and job experiences, have you ever experienced a similar situation? Moreover, have you ever quit or lost a job because you were inflexible and just could not deal with things? Be honest. As we discussed, no matter how much you would like to do the job in a way that makes you more comfortable, you usually have to perform the job in ways that produce the best results, even if you have to leave your comfort zone temporarily to do it.

The Willingness to Be Adaptive

Intellectually, we can all say how much we are flexible or intend to be flexible in our behavior. The fact is, we tend to think we are more adaptable than we really are. The real test comes in *how we feel* emotionally and *how others react to us* when we think we are adapting. For example, think of yourself as a rubber band. At rest, in the unstretched state, you will feel little or no tension or stress—you are in your comfort zone. However, when called upon to stretch out of your state of rest, or comfort zone, you will likely experience some degree of tension or stress. You can definitely feel that you are out of your comfort zone. This is particularly true in moments of conflict or friction when we sense a threat to ourselves. In such times, we tend to retreat even more strongly into our core behavior set, and we amplify those behaviors. For example, under stressful conditions like this:

- A High D might get more aggressive and work for a win-lose outcome.
- A High I might get more emotionally expressive, lose objectivity, and agree on something just to keep the relationship intact.
- A High S might give in on some issue just to avoid any unpleasantness or conflict.
- A High C might go into a defensive, avoiding posture, calculating how their solution is better than another's is.

In other words, we don't filter our behavior by asking, "What's the right thing to do here?" Instead, we act pretty much out of pure emotion.

This is the primary reason people are unwilling to be adaptive. They are just simply unwilling to endure the pain of moving too far out of their comfort zones to do things differently. However, the good news is that the more we do it, the more comfortable we become. In addition, when others sense that we are trying to come their way, generally they tend to respond correspondingly and come our way.

Another reason why many people are not willing to flex their behaviors is that they may have a strong belief in some position or issue, and so, rather than compromise on that, their stubbornness is translated to their behavior as well. Bill Ury, author of *Getting to Yes*, one of the foremost experts on successful negotiating, says that when we feel strongly about something and need to work out disagreements with others, we need to be soft on them as people (adapt!) and hard on issues. To do this requires good self-awareness and emotional control.

The Skill to Be Adaptive

Just being willing to adapt is only half the equation. The other half is knowing what to do to be most effective—the skill of adaptability. As a starting point, I think it would be helpful to describe where people of the various DISC styles would naturally tend to have the most difficulty being adaptive and what they can do to be more adaptive.

High Ds and Adaptability

Remember, High Ds want to shape their environment by overcoming opposition to accomplish results. Therefore, High D, dominance-oriented people may

- exert a controlling, emotionally detached approach in most situations
- want to control others and maintain a formal, business-like approach to things
- overuse a direct, blunt, communication style

- approach things in a competitive manner no matter what the consequences.

In general, High Ds would be more effective if they
- listened more completely and patiently
- showed more concern and empathy for the feelings of others
- understood the effects of their powerful, dominant behavior on others
- exercised more patience and concern for people around them, rather than for the immediate tasks and priorities that drive them
- slowed down a bit to smell the roses.

High Is and Adaptability

High Is want to shape their environment by influencing or persuading others. Therefore, High I influence-oriented people may
- exert a controlling, emotional approach to most situations
- focus on relationships and feelings, over facts and logic
- make quick, emotionally based decisions
- overuse enthusiasm, optimism, and praise.

In general, High Is would be more effective if they
- acted more deliberately and objectively when facing problems and issues
- paid more attention to detail and analyzed things more carefully
- were more emotionally controlled and realistic when dealing with issues and problems
- focused more on results than on how people feel about something.

High Ss and Adaptability

Remember, the High S emphasizes cooperating with others within existing circumstances to carry out tasks. Because of this, the steadiness-oriented High S may

- exert an adaptive, emotional approach to most situations
- focus on relationships and feelings in most situations
- maintain a stable, unchanging approach
- overuse indirectness, sympathy, and toleration of others' shortcomings.

In general, High Ss would be more effective if they

- accepted change and unpredictable situations more readily
- exercised more of a sense of urgency and took the lead more often
- showed more forcefulness and personal strength
- were more direct and confident in offering their opinions.

High Cs and Adaptability

As we know, the High C emphasizes working conscientiously within circumstances to ensure quality and accuracy. Because of this, the conscientiousness-oriented High C may

- exert a subtle or indirect approach in most situations
- approach most things in a businesslike, logical, fact-based manner
- approach most things in a deliberate manner, carefully weighing the pros and cons
- follow key directives and standard operating procedures to the letter.

In general, High Cs would be more effective if they

- changed their slow, analytical pace to accommodate others
- showed more empathy to others' feelings, respecting their personal worth as much as their accomplishments

- acted more spontaneously and took more shortcuts
- decided more quickly to get things moving
- developed a tolerance for conflict.

Adapting to a Work Culture

So far, we've focused on adapting your style one-on-one with another person. However, what do you do to adapt within a work culture where you are not a good fit, e.g., where the prevailing behavioral norms are one way and you are quite different in your approach? For example, I taught a DISC-based team-building session to a corporate staff. It was a very High C group, with a few High Ds sprinkled in. Near the end of the session, each of the participants revealed something of themselves in relation to style. The one High I in the group said, "When I first came here I felt isolated. Everywhere I looked people were plugged into their computers, and didn't make much of an effort to talk to me. It took me six months to realize nobody was mad at me. They were only on-task. Now, with this DISC training, I realize it was nothing personal, but only a bunch of High Cs doing what they do best."

Regardless of the styles at play, perhaps you have seen or experienced a similar situation. What do you do about it? Basically, there are three approaches you might want to consider:

- *Blend*—With this approach you modify your own behavior sufficiently enough to blend into the culture. That means you will move out of your comfort zone and stay there, nearly all of the time. If the move isn't too far, you may only notice a little stress. However, if the move requires you to make a constant stretch or redirection in your behavior, you will likely experience high stress. Long term, this will take its toll in your satisfaction and performance. My own experience outlined in the introduction is an example of this.

- *Augment*—This involves role swapping where, because of some particular behavioral strength, you support others in their role performance. In turn, they might support you. As an example, suppose you have a particularly High D behavioral pattern in a High S-C culture, and one of your peers is a High S. If the High S had the task of negotiating some important outcome, chances are that person would probably dread such a thing because of the perceived conflict involved. However, as a High D, the prospect of going face-to-face in a negotiation session probably would not be a problem for you. Augmentation is a good way for people to be at their best and be comfortable, if only for a short time.

- *Capitalize on Strength*—Everyone, because of style, has certain strengths to bring to the workplace. Moreover, if people are lucky, they can apply those strengths to their best advantage. For example, Leslie, a High S-C friend of mine, works as a personnel manager in an organization with a High D culture. The culture is fast-paced, competitive, and impersonal. Many of the staff call her the chaplain because she is such a good listener and a safety valve for people who want to talk and vent when the high-pressure culture gets too overwhelming. Her strengths of empathy, listening, and showing respect for others are highly prized by her company. She plays a key role.

Identifying the Behavioral Style of Others

One of the most useful skills you can learn is the ability to identify the behavioral style of the people with whom you associate—your family members, your customers, your coworkers, your managers, and others. This will help you avoid the mistake of judging them based purely on their surface behaviors. Instead, you will be able to recognize their behaviors and understand them on another level. You will pretty much know what drives them (their emotional goals) and what turns them off (their emotional fears). Most importantly, you will gain direct clues about how you can manage your own behavior to relate to them most effectively.

When we are around other people who are like us, we have a sense of comfort about them, an intuitive feeling that things feel right. In effect, we have a behavioral kinship with them. We do not need to identify their style, we just know. However, we often meet other people in our daily lives who are very different from us, and wonder, "What's with them?" By learning style identification skills, we can eliminate the guesswork and get off to a good start with them.

As we introduced in Chapter 2, our behaviors—body language, voice tone, and words/priorities—reflect our emotional goals and fears. Given the four DISC tendencies, we tend to express ourselves in unique and identifiable ways. With a little practice, you can identify these surface behaviors in others and quickly identify the style of those people.

In Table 7.1, I summarized the range of behaviors you might typically see in people who have a strong orientation to each of the four behavioral domains. Note that these are typical behaviors, usually seen when people are operating within their comfort zone. However, behaviors can and do vary situationally. As Marston discovered, we tend to behave differently based on how favorable or unfavorable we see our world and how powerful we see ourselves within that world. For example, a High D would probably not exert too much of her dominant, direct style of communication when having lunch with a good friend. However, if the food came late or cold, the natural forceful, direct tendencies of the High D would probably kick in, and she would solve the food problem quickly and directly!

Table 7.1. Typical Behaviors by Style

CHARACTERISTIC	DOMINANCE	INFLUENCE	STEADINESS	CONSCIENTIOUSNESS
BODY LANGUAGE				
Facial	• *Cool, formal*	• *Warm, informal*	• *Warm, informal*	• *Cool, formal*
Eye Contact	• *Sustained*	• *Sustained*	• *Intermittent*	• *Intermittent*
Posture	• *Formal*	• *Informal*	• *Informal*	• *Formal*
Gestures	• *Lots, dominance*	• *Lots, emotion*	• *Restrained*	• *Restrained*
General Makeup	• *Active* • *Fast paced*	• *Active* • *Fast paced*	• *Calm* • *Moderate paced*	• *Calm* • *Moderate paced*
VOICE TONE				
Speech pace	• *Fast*	• *Fast*	• *Slow*	• *Slow*
Volume	• *Loud*	• *Loud*	• *Soft*	• *Soft*
Inflection	• *Some*	• *Lots*	• *Some*	• *Little*
WORDS / PRIORITIES				
General style	• *Direct* • *Questioning*	• *Sociable* • *Accepting*	• *Empathetic* • *Accepting*	• *Analytical* • *Questioning*
Tell vs. Ask	• *More telling*	• *More telling*	• *More asking*	• *More asking*
Focuses On	• *Results*	• *Relationships*	• *Feelings*	• *Correctness*
Expression of Feelings	• *Private*	• *Fully open*	• *Tentatively open*	• *Private*
Risk Tolerance	• *More*	• *More*	• *Less*	• *Less*
Asks Question	• *What?*	• *Who?*	• *How?*	• *Why?*
Response	• *Restless*	• *Enthusiastic*	• *Relaxed*	• *Keeps distance*

Another complication of style identification is that, as you have seen in the behavior patterns described in Chapters 3–6, many people have more than one high behavioral dimension. In effect, their behavior is a blend of the dominant behavioral characteristics of their highest tendencies. These subtleties are not always easy to discern. It is for these reasons—situational behavior and blended behavioral patterns—that style identification is an art, not a science. It is easier to identify the style of some people because their behaviors are consistent and obvious—they are who they are, no matter what. Others, who are more flexible in their style, are more difficult to read. They act differently based on the situation. Usually, one needs to see them in multiple settings and roles over time to get a firm fix on their style. Ultimately, however, if you can be reasonably sure about the one most obvious behavioral tendency you see, you will have enough to go with in planning your adaptability strategy.

To help you build your skills, let's do some style identification. First, a note of caution: we are not analyzing or evaluating people. That is the role of a competent mental health practitioner. Here, we are only identifying the behavior style of others so we can understand them and meet their needs better.

Style Identification Exercise

In this section, I will describe in more behavioral detail some of the people of the various DISC styles that you read about in the case scenarios in Chapters 3–6. Using Table 7.1, as you read the description of each person, try to identify that person's predominant style, and then jot his or her name on the corresponding box in Table 7.2. Wait until you have completed this exercise before going back into the previous chapters to check on their actual styles.

Directions: Write the names of the individuals that you think correspond with their primary behavior tendency. Also, highlight their key style behaviors as you read the descriptions. If you think you have identified a secondary behavioral tendency, place the person's name in that box with a "(2)" after the name.

Table 7.2. Style Identification Chart

The High Ds:	The High Is:
The High Cs:	The High Ss:

- *Warren, the human resources executive*: Warren is very active and focused. He readily sorts out priorities and easily shifts his attention to things that need focus. On the surface, he has a pleasant demeanor, but is quite serious with his engaging, direct eye contact. He has accomplished a lot in a short time, often in the face of strong opposition. He is quite private with his feelings until he trusts you. *Put Warren's name in the correct style box in Table 7.2.*

- *Phillip, the hotel bellman:* Phillip is an enthusiastic, warm person with an engaging smile. He moves quickly and hardly ever stands still. He is very service-minded and loves meeting and being around customers. Above all, he enjoys talking with them about their travels and enjoys recommending places to eat and see while they are in town. He is very animated in his gestures. *Put Phillip's name in the correct style box in Table 7.2.*

- *Pamela, the medical office assistant*: Pamela is a calm, warm, and friendly person who cares about most everyone she meets. She speaks in a moderate pace and usually quite softly. She is most comfortable in small groups and usually avoids large gatherings. She thinks things through carefully before acting and prefers planning things out rather than being spontaneous. She is very sensitive to the plight of people in difficulty and conveys a genuine regard for them in both her words and actions. Unless she is sure of her ground, Pamela usually keeps her opinions to herself. *Put Pamela's name in the correct style box in Table 7.2.*

- *Ray, the training manager:* Ray is low-key, undemonstrative, and cool. He is usually quite serious and holds his emotions to himself. He is very calm and deliberate in his approach to things. He delights in complex, detailed work and prefers to work alone. Before solving a problem or acting on some issue, Ray always seeks to get the full picture through questioning others. He is complete and accurate in most everything he does. *Put Ray's name in the correct style box in Table 7.2.*

- *Larry, the retired police officer:* Larry is an active person who has no difficulty speaking his mind. Except in social environments where he is relaxed, he is usually quite serious and formal. He is quite deliberate before acting on problems or issues. He tends to look you straight in the eye when talking and keeps most things private. He has a strong focus on doing things right and doing them right now. *Put Larry's name in the correct style box in Table 7.2.*

- *Julie, the bank teller:* Julie is a warm, calm, analytical, and cheerful person. Normally, she is not too demonstrative and shuns attention. She usually stays with the tried and true way of doing things. She strives for completeness and correctness. She also plays it safe, avoiding any unnecessary risks. She is a good storyteller and leaves out no details in the telling. Julie is such a routine person, you can almost set your watch by her. *Put Julie's name in the correct style box in Table 7.2.*

- *Judith, the insurance brokerage company owner:* Judith is an enthusiastic, warm, and high-energy person. She loves people. She talks fast, laughs often, and readily expresses her views. You always know she is in the room because, with her louder voice and engaging manner, she usually takes command of any space. She is constantly on the move—doing something or going somewhere. She enjoys the rewards of her work in the form of luxury cars and big homes. Judith can get very serious and direct when she encounters challenges that get in her way. *Put Judith's name in the correct style box in Table 7.2.*

- *Owen, the loss-control consultant:* Owen is a warm, caring, relaxed, and sociable person. He is somewhat restrained in his emotions, but not so much that you do not know him. He is willing to serve the needs of others anytime with little concern for himself. Owen is very patient with people and in performing tasks. He is willing to take risks, but usually prefers to engineer the risk out of things before acting. *Put Owen's name in the correct style box in Table 7.2.*

So, how do you think you did? Now check for the correct answers at the end of this chapter. Perhaps you were at a disadvantage because you could not actually see or hear these people. I can assure you that that makes style identification a lot easier!

If you want to build your style identification skills even more, you may enjoy identifying the style of some of the key people in your own world. Make a list on Table 7.3 of 10 people in your life with whom you interact frequently. Then, think about them and observe them in various settings. You may have to apply multiple readings because their behavior may vary situationally. What behaviors do you see over time? What do you think their style is? Use Table 7.1 and the following questions as a guide for your observations:

- Do they take a more assertive, *telling* approach with others (Ds and Is), or do they take a more *asking* approach (Ss and Cs), going along to get along?
- Are they *warmer* (Ss and Is) or *cooler* (Ds and Cs) in their general demeanor?
- Are they more *casual* (Is and Ss) or more *formal* (Ds and Cs) in their general approach to things?
- Do they talk with a *lot of gesturing* (Is and Ds), or are they *restrained* (Ss and Cs) in their hand movements?
- Do they speak in a *measured* pace (Ss and Cs) or more *rapidly* (Ds and Is)?
- In their messages, do they focus on *results* through action (Ds), *relationships* through influence (Is), *stability* through preparation (Ss), or *correctness* through adherence to standards and analysis (Cs)?
- Do they readily *reveal their feelings* (Is and Ds), or are they *more closed* (Cs and Ss)?

Table 7.3. Behavioral Styles of Key People in My Life

Person	Probable Style 1st Sighting	Probable Style 2nd Sighting	Probable Style 3rd Sighting	Probable Style 4th Sighting

Adapting Your Style to Meet the Needs of Others

As we know, when dealing with others, our tendency is to do what is most natural for us. The adaptive person, however, does what is most appropriate or effective for the relationship or situation at hand. Through seemingly no effort, some people are just unconsciously competent in this skill. They always seem to do the right thing. However, most of us need to think and plan a little to be most effective.

So, let us examine specific ways we can be more adaptive. It starts with observing the behaviors of another, determining the person's style, and then comparing your behavioral similarities and differences. Once this is clear, you should then ask yourself the following questions: In regards to my own behavior, in this situation

- what should I *start doing* that I am not doing now to stretch to something I need to do to be more effective?
- what should I *stop doing* that I am now doing that may not be useful to redirect a strength so that it doesn't get in the way?
- what should I *continue to do* that seems to be working that is a fit for this situation?

Provided you know yourself, these questions should give you direct and clear answers about the approach to use. Sometimes, your behavioral shift may require only minimal effort, like speaking up a little faster or being more serious in your demeanor. At other times, your adaptation may require more in-depth changes like focusing more on detail or listening more patiently.

Sometimes, when you have a lot at stake with another person and you are committed to an effective interpersonal encounter, you may want to commit more time and thought as to how you will adapt. For your convenience, Table 7.4, Behavioral Adaptability Strategy Planner, is suitable for this purpose. You may also download copies of this planner free from my website, www.WeHugintheHallwaysHere.com.

Table 7.4. Behavioral Adaptability Strategy Planner

The Other Person:

Name of person with whom I want to relate most effectively: _____

This person's known or identified DISC style: _____

This person's most usual and prominent behavioral characteristics:

_____

_____

What is my objective in this meeting? (To change? To influence? To make up?)

_____

_____

How might this person likely respond to me?

_____

_____

My Style and Behavior:

My DISC style: _____

My most usual and prominent behavioral characteristics:

_____

_____

What emotional content, if any, am I taking into this situation?

_____

Adaptation Strategy:

Stylewise, how am I like this person? _____

Stylewise, how am I different from this person? _____

Given our similarities and differences, what three behaviors should I stop, start, or continue that will likely produce an effective relationship or meeting?

1. _____

2. _____

3. _____

When will I apply this strategy? _____

How did I do? _____

Adapting to High Ds

To relate most effectively with High Ds, remember they like others to be direct, straightforward, and open to their need for results. When interacting with a High D, be prepared for their blunt and demanding approach, lack of empathy, lack of sensitivity, and little social interaction. High Ds are motivated strongly by

- power and authority
- prestige
- new and varied challenges
- achieving results
- knowing the bottom line
- a wide scope of operations
- direct answers
- freedom from controls, supervision, and detail.

Key adaptability techniques that will work with High Ds include the following:

- Make communication brief and to the point.
- Respect their need for autonomy.
- Be clear about rules and expectations.
- Let them initiate.
- Show your competence.
- Stick to the topic.
- Show independence.
- Eliminate time wasters.

Adapting to High Is

To relate most effectively with High Is, remember they like others to be friendly, emotionally honest, and recognized for their contributions. When interacting with High Is, be prepared for their attempts to persuade or influence you, their need for the limelight, a tendency to exaggerate and oversell ideas, and a vulnerability to perceived rejection. High Is are motivated strongly by

- popularity and recognition
- rewards
- public recognition of their abilities
- people to talk to
- casual, warm relationships
- freedom from control and detail
- approval and friendliness
- identification with others.

Key adaptability techniques that will work with High Is include the following:

- Approach them informally.
- Be relaxed and sociable.
- Let them verbalize thoughts and feelings.
- Keep the conversation light.
- Provide written details to support the conversation.
- Give public recognition for individual accomplishments.
- Use humor.

Adapting to High Ss

To relate most effectively with High Ss, remember they like others to be relaxed, agreeable, cooperative, and appreciative. When interacting with High Ss be prepared for their friendly approach, resistance to change, difficulty prioritizing, and difficulty with deadlines. High Ss are strongly motivated by

- the status quo
- security
- happy and calm relationships
- standardized procedures
- sincerity
- time and support to adjust to change
- genuine appreciation, not necessarily in public
- low-key recognition for service
- an opportunity to specialize.

Key adaptation strategies that will work with High Ss include the following:

- Communicate in a low-key, friendly manner.
- Be logical and systematic in your approach.
- Provide a consistent and secure environment.
- Let them know how things will be done.
- Show sincere appreciation.
- Show their importance to the organizational good.
- Let them move slowly into change.

Adapting to High Cs

To relate most effectively with High Cs, remember they like others to minimize socializing, give details, adhere to high standards, and value accuracy. When interacting with High Cs be prepared for their discomfort with ambiguity, resistance to vague or general information, desire to double check, and little need for affiliation with others. High Cs are strongly motivated by

- limited exposure/risk
- a reserved, business-like environment

- references and verification
- the opportunity to demonstrate expertise
- no sudden changes
- personal autonomy
- personal attention to their objectives
- selective involvement.

Key adaptability techniques that will work with High Cs include the following:

- Be tactful and emotionally reserved.
- Give clear expectations and deadlines.
- Show dependability.
- Show loyalty.
- Allow precedent to be a guide.
- Be precise and focused.
- Value high standards.

Chapter Summary

Adaptability is the skill we use to modify our comfort zone behaviors temporarily to deal most effectively with another person or situation. It may involve redirecting a strength that could get in the way or stretching to a behavior we do not normally display. Whether we adapt or not is a choice we make. However, sometimes you do not have a choice in the matter. For example, your job survival may depend on how well you can adapt to a situation. Therefore, you do it. In other cases, where there is less at stake, you may prefer to act purely out of your comfort zone, even though you do not produce a desired outcome. In most cases, unless you are experienced and skillful at interpersonal flexibility, being adaptive can be stressful because when we adapt we give up something of ourselves (emotional security) to produce a positive result.

However, to apply an old expression—no pain, no gain. You will have to decide whether it is worth it.

The first step in being adaptable is to know yourself. The next step is to know and anticipate the style needs of the other person. Then, with a little planning, you can make a few adjustments in your behavior that will show flexibility and will likely lead to the results you want. In most cases, people who see you as trying to relate with them effectively will make an effort to come your way as well.

Some Things to Think About

Who are the most adaptable people you know? How do they show their adaptability? How does their adaptability affect their interpersonal relationships with you and others?

_____

_____

_____

_____

How do you think others would rate your adaptability? Low? Medium? High? Why would they rate it as such?

_____

_____

_____

_____

Can you think of a time recently when you went out of your comfort zone and adapted your behavior to meet the needs of a particular situation? Why did you do it? What was the result?

_____

_____

_____

_____

What prevents you from being adaptive? Is it your *lack of ability* to do so, or is it your *unwillingness* to do so? What few things could you do to improve your general adaptability?

_____

_____

_____

_____

Are there some people who you just cannot deal with and find it difficult to adapt to their needs? Who are they? What is it about them that makes a good relationship so difficult? What specific thing(s) can you do to change things for the better?

_____

_____

_____

_____

A Final Thought

At the beginning of the book I wrote, "If I can help you make a good career decision, or help you avoid making a bad one, I will have succeeded in my goal." I hope this book has helped you, whether you are just starting your career or are more advanced on your career journey.

It is no secret that personal career management is a daunting process. How do you pick the right job or career? How can you be sure that you have made a good decision? How do you adjust if you are in a difficult situation? There are so many questions, so many unknowns, and so many opportunities. The critical issue is to know thyself. Your career research, personal assessments, job and life experiences, and personal reflection will lead you to right answers.

As I have stated in this book, your personal temperament, or behavioral style, is one of the most important things to consider in managing your career. Your style is a direct reflection of your emotional goals and fears; they are major motivators. If you can get into work and work cultures that are a reasonably good fit for you, you will be more motivated and you will probably be an effective performer. However, if you find yourself in a job that is a bad fit, try to understand your situation better and work to improve things. Ultimately, you may even choose to change jobs or organizations.

This brings to mind the discovery that Richard Lieder, noted author and career development practitioner, made in his work. He asked a group of retired seniors what they would do over again if they could relive their lives. Their answers are very much in tune with what we are saying here. They said they would *take stock more often*, to assure that their lives reflected their goals, needs and values; and they said they would *take more risks* to act on things they wanted, even though there was no guarantee of success. Assessing your needs, finding the fit and acting on your intentions may lead to your own version of "we hug in the hallways here." I certainly hope so.

Answers to the Style Identification Exercise

- Warren, High D, *Developer* pattern
- Phillip, High I, *Promoter* pattern
- Pamela, High S, *Specialist* pattern
- Ray, High C, *Objective Thinker* pattern
- Larry, High D-C, *Creative* pattern
- Julie, High C-S, *Perfectionist* pattern
- Judith, High D-I, *Inspirational* pattern
- Owen, High S-I *Agent* pattern

Appendix A

Resources for More Reading about Behavioral Style and Career-Related Topics

Bolles, Richard Nelson. *What Color Is Your Parachute? A Practical Manual for Job-Hunters and Career-Changers*. Ten Speed Press: Berkley, 2006. *This book has been a job-hunting classic for over three decades and is updated every year. Bolles takes the readers through a series of readings and exercises that help them consider all aspects of the career or job-search process.*

Gale, Linda. *Discover What You're Good At: A Complete Career System That Lets You Test Yourself to Discover Your Own True Abilities*. Fireside: New York, 1998. *This useful book enables you to identify not only your interests, but also your innate talents and potential skills, and then match your career strengths to many of the more than 1,100 jobs described in detail. It is a useful resource to supplement the behavioral style-related aspects of your career search.*

Goleman, Daniel. *Emotional Intelligence: Why It Can Matter More Than IQ.* Bantam Books: New York, 1995. *Goleman's book opened a completely new dialogue about the role and importance of emotions in human interaction and success. In contrast to traditional IQ measures of cognitive ability, emotional intelligence includes self-awareness and impulse control, persistence, zeal and self-motivation, empathy, and social deftness. Knowing your DISC style contributes to emotional intelligence.*

Merrill, David W. and Roger E. Reid. *Personal Styles & Effective Performance.* Chilton Book Company: Radnor, PA, 1981. *Merrill and Reid are important researchers and practitioners in the field of applied behavioral science. As compared to DISC, they have created a different style model, called social style. Social style is determined by assessing one's assertiveness and responsiveness behaviors. As with DISC, the resulting profile is helpful in self-understanding and in practicing interpersonal versatility. The book features an in-depth treatment of social style and how to apply it for personal effectiveness.*

Pearsall, Paul. *The Last Self-Help Book You'll Ever Need.* Basic Books: New York, 2005. *As a psychotherapist for over 40 years, Dr. Pearsall has discovered and offers in this book some valuable suggestions for how we can help ourselves. He also shows how to be most effective in relationships by being more in touch with others and focusing on their feelings and needs. Pearsall's thinking and suggestions align well with the notion in this book that behavioral adaptability takes commitment and skill.*

Ritchey, Tom, with Alex Axelrod. *I'm Stuck, You're Stuck: Break Through to Better Work Relationships and Results by Discovering Your DiSC® Behavioral Style.* Barrett-Koehler Publishers, Inc.: San Francisco, 2002. *Ritchey's book focuses on how to create and sustain good working relationships with others. It gives an in-depth treatment of the dynamics and characteristics of DiSC® and how to use that knowledge to be most interpersonally adaptive.*

Straw, Julie, with Alison Brown Cerier. *The 4-Dimensional Manager: DiSC® Strategies for Managing Different People in the Best Ways.* Berrett-Koehler Publishers, Inc.: San Francisco, 2002. *The premise of this book is that one managerial style can't help people with four different working styles make the most of their strengths and overcome their limitations and roadblocks to performance. Straw offers tips and techniques for managers to manage people of all DiSC® styles most effectively.*

Appendix B

Distribution of DiSC® Classical Profile Patterns in the General Population[1]

Classical Pattern	DiSC® Component(s)	% of reference group[1]
Achiever	Sd	1
Agent	Si	2
Appraiser	Ic	4
Counselor	Is	5
Creative	DC	18
Developer	D	7
Inspirational	DI	11
Investigator	Sdc	1
Objective Thinker	C	7
Perfectionist	SC	16
Persuader	Id	5
Practitioner	Cis	5
Promoter	I	8
Result-Oriented	Di	8
Specialist	S	2

Note: The DiSC® components cited here have a mix of upper case and lower case letters. The Classical Patterns with *equally high* DiSC® components, such as the DC pattern, have two uppercase letters. Those behavioral dimensions are equally high in intensity. The lowercase letters, such as d in the Id pattern, represent a lower intensity behavioral dimension. While a part of the Classical Pattern, it represents behavior lower in intensity and secondary to the primary dimension.

Source: *DiSC® Facilitator Report*, Inscape Publishing, 2008. Used with permission.

1. The reference group for this distribution came from a sample of over 20,000 men and women who have taken an online DiSC® profile for a variety of purposes. The distribution of race in this sample was 12 percent African American, 5 percent Asian American, 74 percent Caucasian, 7 percent Hispanic, and 2 percent Native American. Gender was evenly distributed and all individuals in the sample were above the age of 18. Note that compared to the general population, this sample contains a large number of managers and professionals.

© 2004 by Inscape Publishing, Inc. All rights reserved. Everything DiSC is a registered trademark of Inscape Publishing, Inc.

Share Your Story!

Dear Reader,

My goal in writing this book was to give you helpful information about how to make a "good fit" job choice or career decision based on your behavioral style—or to help you avoid making a bad decision. I hope that I have succeeded in this goal.

However, I'll never know unless I hear from you. If you have a few moments, would you be willing to send me a note, fax, or an email to let me know of your experiences in applying what you have learned in the book? I would appreciate it so much. Thanks. You can either send your story to me at:

Roger E. Wenschlag
Performance Solutions
4829 30th Avenue South
Suite 200
Minneapolis, MN 55417

Email: Rwenschlag@comcast.net
612-721-2610
(Fax) 612-724-1469

Or you can contact me via my website:
www.WeHugInTheHallwaysHere.com

Get More Information or Dig Deeper!

For support on your journey, please visit us at:

www.WeHugInTheHallwaysHere.com.

On this website you can:

- Order more copies of *We Hug in the Hallways Here*
- Obtain a free sample of a DISC style report
- Complete an online assessment and obtain your own DISC style report.
- Obtain the latest support materials
- Download forms that appear in the book
- Download the book's table of contents
- Contact us for special book orders and needs